The Man with a Steel Guitar

A Portrait of Ambition, Desperation, and Crime

The Man with

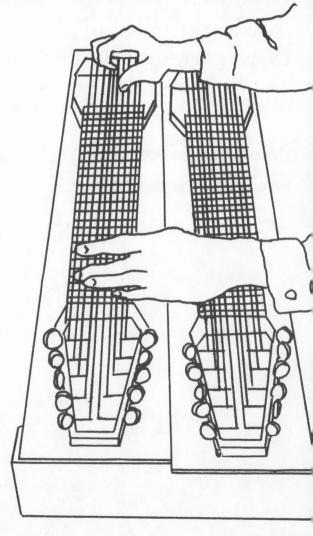

Steel Guitar

A Portrait of Ambition,
Desperation, and Crime

Norman Greenberg

Foreword by Stuart Palmer

University Press of New England
Hanover, New Hampshire and London, England
1980

University Press of
New England

Sponsoring Institutions
Brandeis University
Clark University
Dartmouth College
University of New Hampshire
University of Rhode Island
Tufts University
University of Vermont

Drawings by Anne Kachergis

Library of Congress Catalog Card Number 79-63084
International Standard Book Number 0-87451-175-5
Printed in the United States of America

Library of Congress Cataloging in Publication data
will be found on the last printed page of this book.

And I said, "Give it to me." She's pushin' on the bag
and I'm pullin' on it. And I had the gun in my
hand, and I'm tryin' to get the bag out of there but
it's stuck, there's too much money in the thing.
And I'm sayin', "Give it to me."

—WARREN HART

Lately in a wreck of a California ship, one of the pas-
sengers fastened a belt about him with two hundred
pounds of gold in it, with which he was afterwards
found at the bottom. Now, as he was sinking—had
he the gold? Or had the gold him?

—JOHN RUSKIN

Contents

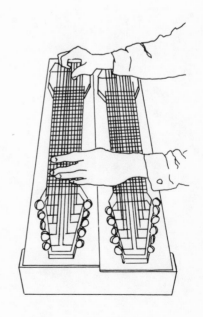

Foreword

The life history has had a long and honorable role both in and outside social science, particularly the life history of the person labeled "criminal offender." The noncriminal activity of the person so labeled far outweighs the criminal activity in his total life experience; he is primarily a group creature, a social being with vast and complex experience in the family and community, often in school and at work, and certainly at play. The offender has the basic yearnings, strivings, fears, and hopes that are common to us all. Like most of us, he not only is formed by the culture and the social system, but contributes to cultural and social change.

It is through understanding the relationships among individuals, groups, social systems, and cultural customs and values that we come to know ourselves and our society. The full-scale life history is one means to that understanding, for it brings us into intimate contact with an individual in a way that enlarges our appreciation of the processes that make us human. Norman Greenberg and Warren Hart have revealed many of the influences that operate to produce, in one life, a series of crimes and a return to noncriminal activity. In so doing they have contributed to the corpus of life histories that illumines the human condition. They have shown that the study of one life can be as far-reaching and as broad and deep in conception as the study of a whole society. They have also provided an artful and sensitive demonstration that qualitative sociology can be as conducive as quantitative sociology to understanding social life.

November 1979   STUART PALMER
University of New Hampshire   *Professor of Sociology*

Preface

The New Hampshire State Prison is an austere, one-hundred-year-old red brick building surrounded on three sides by a high brick wall. The entrance to the prison is a green metal door facing a parking lot. To enter, the visitor presses a buzzer and waits for a guard to peer out and then open the door. Inside on the first floor is a small foyer where some prison handicrafts—various objects of wood and leather—are on display. A guard dressed in a blue uniform waits behind a counter.

To go beyond the anteroom, a visitor must fill out a visitor's pass, place personal effects such as wallet and keys in a locker, and wait for permission to enter to come from somewhere up above. If permission is granted, the visitor walks through a metal detector and stands before a massive door of iron bars, beyond which is an ascending staircase. This is the first of the barred iron doors; like all the rest, it is always locked. The visitor pushes on it to signal a guard up in the control room and waits for a buzzer to sound before trying to open the door.

At the top of the stairway is the control room of the prison. It is encased in bullet-proof glass; the visitor must speak to the guard through a little metal cage and pass papers to him through a depressed slot in the way that money usually is passed to a bank teller. To the right are the staff's offices behind another barred iron door. To the left is the visiting room filled with long wooden tables—two iron doors away. Behind the control room are the cell blocks—three more barred iron doors away.

I visited the prison approximately three times a week, for about three hours each time, throughout the summer of 1975, to interview the man identified in this book as Warren Hart for the purpose of creating a life history. The prison warden at that time, Raymond Helgemoe, had agreed to this project and had agreed to introduce me to several inmates. Hart, a thin man about five feet nine inches tall, with sandy brown hair, was the second inmate I met. I chose to work with him simply because of his apparent interest in and enthusiasm for this project; I knew nothing about his background until his story unfolded through my questioning. We sat opposite each other at a small wooden table in a kitchen in the staff's wing of the prison. I brought along a tape recorder and, with his agreement, taped most of our conversation.

I had studied various life histories as well as novels with a first-person point of view; in addition, I had developed a simple typology of human aspiration and reaction. In consequence I decided to prepare a straightforward, more or less chronological, account of the man's life based on vivid descriptions of a series of crucial events—the beginnings and conclusions of love, work, and any other subjectively important activity (in this case, religion). To obtain these descriptions, I questioned Hart generally about such experiences and asked him successive questions until a scene was virtually recreated. I was primarily interested in recreating dialogue; when he told me he could not remember the exact words, I would say, "Tell me approximately what was said. It is not really necessary for the words to be exactly what was said at the time." I would also continually but indirectly ask him to describe his feelings and thoughts at the time, by suggesting possible thoughts and emotions and asking if he had felt that way at the time or, if not, why not. I would say, for instance, "Many people in these circumstances would have done such-and-such; why didn't you?" I was always careful to react decently to what Hart said: to treat seriously and with respect what was confidential or serious or sad, and to relax and enjoy certain events he too thought were sheer comedy, including much that went on during his crime spree. I also took care at times to restrain my questions so that he could pursue the direction and momentum of his thinking. We explored first his decision to commit crime, then his account of the crimes, then his life before the crimes, and finally his experience in court and prison.

By the time our interviews ended in the fall of 1975, I had approximately fifty hours of conversation on tape. Shortly after each conversation, I reviewed the tape and edited and rearranged the material in a preliminary way, eliminating my own comments and questions as well as comments of his that were redundant or not relevant to the story. I also enlarged certain of his answers (such as simple yeses or noes) so that they would contain my question or otherwise be more clear, and rearranged his comments to fit the chronological sequence. Finally, I changed all names and certain other identifying information appearing in the life history, such as the title and contents of a popular song he claimed to have co-authored.

The product of these efforts—this life history—is rich with the atmosphere of contemporary American life and sentiments. It is filled with the kind of bittersweet irony that is so common in real life and so rarely captured in fiction.

This book has much to teach us. First of all, it shows conversion to crime in adulthood, whereas most criminal biographies tell of people whose criminality began when they were very young; motivation therefore is more complex and conscious here than in other accounts. Second, it relates very amateurish, even comical, attempts at crime while other books tell of a minority of expert criminals. Finally, the life history illustrates numerous sociological and psychological themes besides crime. An example is the ambition for success which is a very prominent theme of this story.

Durham, New Hampshire
December, 1979

Acknowledgments

A number of people have helped me in the preparation of this book, and I wish to thank them.

Most of all I am grateful to the man known here by the name Warren Hart for patiently and eloquently revealing to me the story of his life.

I want to thank Raymond Helgemoe, former Warden of the New Hampshire State Prison, for introducing and enabling me to meet with Hart. I appreciate also the advice and encouragement of Professors Stuart Palmer, Arnold Linsky, Howard Shapiro, Gerald Pyne, and William Jones, all of the University of New Hampshire.

Only my wife, Susan, could have given me the confidence, energy, and perspective necessary to carry this project to its conclusion.

The Man with a Steel Guitar

A Portrait of Ambition, Desperation, and Crime

Prologue

I went to the prison the next morning after the trial and the sentencing. That was May of 1970. Two deputy sheriffs came for me. One of them was an old-timer and the other was a young guy. I was just sitting and waiting for them in my cell in the county jail. I had packed up and was waiting to go. They said, "Get ready. It's time to go." Then they searched me, and I was handcuffed.

The sheriffs' cars in that country are white with a gold star on the door—"Sheriff" printed underneath it. The two sheriffs rode in the front and I rode alone in the back. There was a heavy mesh screen between the rear of the car and the front. And you're locked in and you can't unlock the doors from the inside. I sat alone behind them in the car, and I must have sat there in some kind of a shock because I can't remember thinking anything or feeling anything, just watchin' the towns and the countryside roll by, all the towns I had known since childhood. The nightmare playin' itself out.

It was about noon, I think, when we got to the prison. The guard who opened the door was a lieutenant. And, well, the sheriffs announced that they had arrived and they had the papers from the courts—the commitment order—and all of those things. They signed papers saying that I was delivered.

I was brought into a small shower room. They had clothes racks in there, with street clothes as well as prison clothes. I was told to take a shower and then to change because I was still in my own clothes from court. I was disinfected with some kind of solvent. It was in a blue can with holes punched into the top. I don't know what it was. It was a cold and dismal place, damp, all stone and steel, and the person processing me was very formal and had a standard form of description for my personal property. All of my personal things were taken away from me and recorded on the form. Then I was issued clothing—prison jacket, prison shirt, prison jeans, prison shoes.

First they put you into a quarantine cell for two weeks. The reason for it is so they can come and get you when they want you for processing, like the photographing and fingerprints and interviews by the mental health people and your physical. All kinds of things go on in those two weeks. That's your quarantine time before you're assigned work in prison industries and you're put into one of the regular cells.

The cells are bad and old; the prison in New Hampshire is very old. There's no fresh air and you have no control over your ventilation or heat. Even the air you breathe is controlled by the guards. It's damp and cold usually—just granite walls, brick floors, and granite ceilings. There's a bunk just wide enough for one person, a desk, a chair. The desk serves as a dresser. A toilet sits beside your head day and night.

When I first went there, there was a lights-out policy at eleven o'clock, and you might be in the middle of writing a letter or studying or trying to do something and the lights would go out. You had no control over that either. That was especially hard on me because, being a musician, I was used to the night life. So for a long time I stayed up through the night, sittin' back on my bed in the dark, thinking back on the mistakes I had made and all I had lost.

Part 1

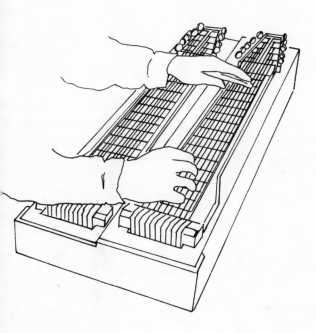

1

I was born in 1934 in Dover, New Hampshire. Dad was a carpenter and machinist. He had skills along those lines, but I don't know exactly what work he was into when I was born. I know he did work as a carpenter in my youth, and during the war he worked at the navy yard, working on submarines.

I was the oldest boy, the second child. I had an older sister. She was eight years old when I was born. And it's been told me that my mother wasn't really supposed to have any more children. The doctor advised against it. I guess her health was in jeopardy if she had any more children. That's the reason for the eight years between my oldest sister and myself. She just decided she wanted more children regardless of the risk. They had me, and then there was five others. There was seven children, which turned out to be a pretty good family for somebody who was supposed to have just one child.

They were both alcoholics, both my father and my mother. They'd drink at home on the weekends. They both worked, and on the weekends they'd drink. It seemed to affect 'em in different ways. Sometimes they'd get violent and my father would hit my mother, and I didn't like that. When I was a youngster growin' up, I hated him for it. And I hated him probably until I was, oh, sometime in my teens, had children of my own, and got out into life. I love my father dearly today and I have for a long, long time.

When my father'd get violent like that, my mother would get away from him. She had an automobile and a license. If he was gonna be mean or somethin', she'd wait until he went somewhere to do somethin', she'd take all of the kids and go away.

It was an unsettled kind of life, but I don't want to paint a real terribly bad, gloomy picture of that because it wasn't that bad either. A lot of times it was good. The drinkin' was confined mostly to the weekends. Dad worked pretty regularly and he limited his drinkin' to the weekends and not every weekend neither. We done a lot of huntin' and fishin' and sports together.

I'd steal a taste of their beer sometimes, and I liked the taste of it. I think all children do. I probably thought that was why they were drinkin'. I don't remember clearly.

I don't think they were discontented with what they had. They were just social drinkers. Dad liked to party a lot, and Mom drank so she could be with him.

Overall it was a real happy childhood. There was a lot of love, security, a lot of hard work and discipline.

My dad really loved music. He played the harmonica. He always had a drawer full of 'em. He was pretty good at it. I'd always get one of his. I guess I ruined all of his harmonicas, blowin' 'em. Like if I'd eat pancakes and have syrup in my mouth or somethin', I wouldn't have sense to know it would ruin the harmonica. But I learned to play it.

Now, there used to be a school in the country, down on Beckworth Road, the schoolhouse. There was six grades in one room with one teacher, and they later turned it into a community club, the Piscataqua Community Club, of which I was a member when I was a kid growin' up and I played harmonica. I was in the early teens, sixth grade maybe. And Joe Marini played guitar, Jimmy Wilson sang. We had a little band when we was kids, and they hired us to play for their dances.

My mother loved to tune in Wheeling on the radio on Friday nights. That's the only time you could get country music out of Wheeling, West Virginia, on Friday nights. I listened to that music and I learned the songs, years ago. I always liked the five-string banjo and the mountain music and the fiddles.

We had, in our house, one of those player pianos that you put rolls on and pump with your feet. Dad loved that thing. Like sometimes when he was drinkin', it wasn't always bad, we'd all

8

get around that piano and he'd play them rolls and sing with the kids. It was fun. I don't know where he got that player piano. It was something he wanted so he went and bought it. They had money. They weren't rich but they weren't poor either, during the Second World War.

One time, WCOP—now, we didn't even get that station—put a show touring around, back in the forties. And Dusty Rhodes was with the WCOP show that come into the city of Dover and played at the city hall. And there was a young fellow playin' steel guitar for him, a man who was a real crackerjack. That was the first time I'd ever seen a steel guitar. And he was very, very good on it. It fascinated me, and I went up on stage afterwards and talked with him.

I didn't get a high school education. I dropped out of high school. I got in an argument with my English teacher, and she failed me because of a book report that I hadn't got in. Even though my grades were real high in that class, she failed me, and I got bitter over that. I didn't think that I should've been failed. I should've maybe been punished or disciplined for my incompleteness or been required to make it up. But she failed me. And that kept me back from goin' into my senior year of high school. In my junior year I quit because of her.

She was at least partially deaf, if not totally deaf. She had a hearing aid. She was an old lady and I think the day for her to be teaching had long passed, way before I got into her class. She wasn't very tolerant of children's pranks. Some of the guys would tease her, and they'd hiss. And there'd be this hissin' sound, and she'd mess with her hearin' aid. She'd think it was her hearin' aid. They'd torment her. And she couldn't take it. She just wasn't up to it, that's all. She was a character. She'd stomp around and holler and stuff, and glare at people. She'd tell 'em to come back after class and nobody'd show up. She wasn't very effective. She liked the kids that got all of their reports in on time and didn't write out in the margins and done everythin' strictly according to her rules. And the funny thing is, I liked English. She was my English teacher.

She was drivin' me frantic. Like we had to read *Ivanhoe,* and I couldn't stand that. I wouldn't read it today, I think it's trash.

Nothin' so borin' in your life as readin' *Ivanhoe*. He'd describe a character, in the book, and he'd describe what the guy was wearin'. And when he got to the belt, he'd tell you where the belt was made and who made that. It's a classic example of stupidity, I think, *Ivanhoe*. Now, the theme of the story might be good. He could've wrote a real nice story if he didn't get bogged down so much in description. But it was totally borin'. It never got to the action. Who cares where the threads were made for the clothes and who raised the sheep where the wool came from? It was ridiculous. And these are the things I resented.

I'd never do a book report on *Ivanhoe*. I just didn't turn it in. She kept tellin' me to get it in, and then she failed me on it, one marking grade. For that, she failed me for the whole year.

I probably thought about dropping out of school before then, but that was the frosting on the cake. That gave me good reason to. When I saw that F, I didn't think it was fair, 'cause I had got good grades on the tests and things like that. I had done plenty of work in the class. That was my only failure, that one book report. And when I saw it, I said, "That's fine, That's good. That's just what I been waitin' for. Stuff it. I don't really need you. Hell with it all." And I quit. And I went to work.

I told my mother and my father I wasn't goin' back. Well, they felt bad about it and tried to talk me out of it. And I wouldn't listen. I was of the age then when I wasn't about to listen. I was ready to leave home over it too. If necessary, I would've. But they didn't push it that hard. The headmaster of the high school did call my parents and asked them to try to have me reconsider 'cause I had the potential to be a good student and they wanted me to stay in there. But I just wouldn't do it.

I think I was workin' with my uncle at that time, installin' lightnin' rods. And I liked that, 'cause I was outside and I was doin' things that interested me. I worked on my uncle's crew. He didn't own the business. I learned to do some steeplejack work, like we put the lightning rods on White City Church. That's a church in White City, Massachusetts, and it's ninety feet from the eaves, and I was climbin' around on that thing. It's seasonal work, and I probably worked up until the winter.

I don't think I done much durin' the winter. I was workin' for my family, gettin' wood in and things like that. That's when I started playin' the steel guitar, teachin' myself.

The steel guitar is an instrument that you sit at and you slide a bar on the strings and you use finger picks and foot pedals, you use both your feet and both hands. It's the Hawaiian sound, but it's far from that today. It has tremendous range on it, in pitch.

Billy Walker, he had a steel guitar. Him and his sister used to have a radio show. She was a terrific singer and is a terrific singer today. And Billy used to play the guitar and sing at the garage where the kids used to have their hot rods at and fix 'em up and work on cars and things. He owned the garage, and he'd play the guitar and he'd sing. And his sister, Leena Mae, she'd sing. It was country and western, bluegrass, and old folk songs. And I really liked it. And the kids would sit around and listen. We'd sing along too, but mostly we'd listen.

I bought the steel guitar off him. That was my first steel guitar. I bought an amplifier and a steel guitar. It was a cheap one, little six-string student guitar. I'd fool around with it at the garage, but I couldn't make it sound good. It sounded horrible. I don't know how it came that I bought it. I just wanted it, and I asked him if he'd sell it to me, and he did. And I took it home and learned how to play it. I drove my parents crazy with it. I developed on it pretty good, though, and I got popular at parties.

When I started to play the steel guitar, in the fifties, guys like Webb Pierce were gettin' popular. They called him the Wanderin' Boy. He had a lot of hit records on wanderin'. And Kitty Wells was the Queen of Country Music.

2

I got into sports, softball league, and working' for Eastern Air Devices and playin' ball for them. A bunch of guys I was playin' ball with, they were some of the ones I played music with, decided to go to California. I was nineteen then. We were kind of popular then. We was gettin' in our late teens. And we had a good ball team, we was startin' to play music pretty good and had a lot of girl friends. You known, we were the popular, real popular, guys. Adventuresome. Most of 'em were adventuresome type people. I went out to California with Billy Cadosi, Joe Marini, and Frank Beaulieu. I heard Beaulieu later committed suicide.

We went to California 'cause there wasn't much opportunity in the east coast, especially the Dover area, unless you wanted to work in a shoe shop or the tanneries. And that wasn't for me because I could see guys goin' into tanneries and startin' out at $1.47 an hour and somebody who'd been there fifteen years only earning $.10 an hour more. So that's not much incentive or much to look forward to. You didn't have to be a financial expert to see that there wasn't much of a future in that.

We didn't have any destination in mind when we went out there to California. We got on the Pennsylvania Turnpike, we picked up Route 66 and went all the way Route 66 to Albuquerque, New Mexico, the Texas Panhandle, out across Arizona into California, through the foothills. We got into the grape-fields. We were starvin', so we ate grapes. And then we pulled off the freeway and wound up in Huntington Beach. We settled down in Long Beach.

That was 1954. I was nineteen and 1A on the draft. And the Korea situation, you know what that was in '54. It was rough. We all had trouble gettin' a job because of our age. Nobody wanted to hire us and train us for anything and then us be drafted into the war, so we couldn't get work.

We was starvin'. We couldn't get nothing' except what we could steal, to eat. Like if somebody had six quarts of milk on their doorstep in the mornin', we'd take one or two and we'd drink that. We couldn't work. And we had no income. I had people come right out and tell me, "Yeh, I'm gonna do some hirin' but why should I hire you? You're nineteen years old, and I'll just get ya trained and you'll be gone." We had to steal to eat. Like if we'd go in and buy two items in a store, we'd steal six. But it was always food. We lived that way.

Not all the guys could steal. Some of 'em was too scared to, afraid they'd get caught or somethin'. Those of us who did have talents used 'em. It's a good thing we did or I don't know what would have happened to us. And we'd eat out of the orchards, like I said, we'd get into the grapes.

One time I was so hungry, me and one of the other guys went into a restaurant and ordered a meal. We didn't have a penny in our pocket. And people kept comin' in, so we had to keep orderin' stuff. It seemed like every time we'd get ready to go, somebody else would come in so we had to order somethin' else. I couldn't hardly stand to eat any more. And I'm quite sure the girl knew what we was doin' after a while. We kept orderin' stuff. When she'd ask us did we want anything else or did we want the bill or somethin', we'd order somethin' else. So she finally caught on. She went out to the back room and stayed out there awhile, and we ran out and ran and ran hard. And we got down on the beach and got sick and lost the dinner. So it didn't do us any good.

It was pretty rough. I wouldn't send home for money from my people. Once in a while maybe my sister or somebody'd send a money order. But we didn't want 'em to worry about us or think we was havin' trouble, so we couldn't ask for too much. Once in a while we'd take turns sendin' home for money. That would keep us goin'.

We were like sober people on skid row, if you can visualize it, and young instead of bein' old derelicts. But it was because of the war and because we couldn't get work. We were starvin'. We were livin' on the beach. We'd drive around in Joe's car. We could just scrape up enough money to get gas and look for work. We'd live on the beach. And then we found out we couldn't do that very long. The mist would come in and we'd wake up soppin' wet and cold in the mornin'. We'd have to wait till the sun come up to dry us off. We'd sneak into YMCA's and take showers. We'd keep clean that way or if we couldn't do that, sometimes we'd sneak into gas station rest rooms and clean up in there. So we didn't get grubby. We stayed clean. It was an adventure.

We'd pick up part-time jobs too, at the Y. Like people would want a day laborer, just for one day or somethin'. We did earn some money that way. Whenever we could, we would. Jobs like tearin' down an old building. I got a job for Polk Company workin' on the city directory, enumeratin'. I think they give ya five cents a name. That was interestin'. People don't want to tell ya what they're doin'. Guys threatenin' to knock me down the stairs, everything else. I'd question these people and some of 'em would get pretty hostile. Like if a guy's hidin' out from the law or somethin', he don't want some creep comin' around writin' all the information down—his name and where he works. I ran into all kinds of situations. Dogs would chase me.

3

We started goin' to this mission. We found this mission where we could get a supper if we'd listen to the preachin'. These were Pentecostal people, and I'd never seen any before. They'd raise their hands and holler and shout, speakin' in tongues and doin' all kinds of things. I'd be laughin'. I'd stay away in the back because it made me laugh. But I wanted the soup. The other guys laughed too. They didn't help me much. We was kind of silly and young and we hadn't seen nothin' like that before.

The old bums were there too. They were comin' for the handout. I guess that's how we got turned on to the mission—bein' on the street, we heard the people talk about it. They said, "You oughta come down. You have to go through the service but at least you can get a bowl of soup." One night we were lined up for soup, and this old bum, I'll never forget him. I couldn't tell ya what he looked like, but I remember what he said. He was big, a tall guy, a big stomach on him. He wasn't goin' to the mission, he was just there for the chow anyway. And we was in line, gettin' our food. And, very indignantly, he looked in his bowl of soup, and he says, "What? No meat in the soup tonight!" As if he had paid five dollars for the plate. I thought that was pretty funny.

Brother Bob Hutton was the founder of that mission. His wife was Sister June, Sister June Hutton, and they had eleven kids.

She was a minister too. She later died of cancer, left Brother Bob alone with all them kids. I started to get to know Bob and June. They were very friendly. They welcomed us. I didn't laugh any more, 'cause I felt like I was laughin' at them.

I got to love Bob and June Hutton very much and became a member of the mission, got a job through them at Pacific Greyhound in Long Beach handlin' freight, and began contributing to the mission. I began to take the religion pretty serious.

One night an evangelist was speaking at the mission, and some people come down from another church to visit. They do that a lot out in California. One of 'em was a teenage girl and she was with her parents and her grandmother and her kid sister. And I noticed the girl was pretty good-looking. She had a nice face and a nice figure. At that time I was playing the steel guitar in the church, with the pastor's wife. That night she was playing the piano, and maybe one of my buddies was playing the guitar. After the service there was coffee and doughnuts and a little socializing, so I zeroed in on her. But I wouldn't zing right over like a bee after a flower. I talked to Harry, and I talked to Bob, and I talked to Sue, and I worked my way over to her. I spoke to her and said I noticed her enjoying the services. Then maybe I talked about the music and found out she played piano. Or her stepfather, part of his testimony was to sing a song with her mother, a duet type thing, and play guitar. I rapped about that, something that they couldn't or she couldn't be suspicious about. I asked if they enjoyed the services or if they come down there very often, did they plan on comin' back there again, and I somehow let her know that I'd be interested in seein' her again. I didn't just go up to her and say, "Hey, babe, let's go out." I know some guys do that and it works for them, but that's not my style. I was bein' slick. I should have slicked right out the door. Then, when I saw her a second time, I got into more detail, like it's rough livin' at the mission and you miss home and you haven't had a good meal for a long time.

I didn't have nobody else, and I was 3,000 miles away from home, and I was hurtin'. I was lonesome and I was without many friends my own age and not gettin' any dates, not livin' the way I was. Christ, it was like I was out on the desert, you know. So she was very attractive for all those reasons, and she wasn't an ugly girl at all. She was a good-lookin' girl. And then the relationship developed to the point where we called it love. Now, by my definitions of love, I wouldn't call it that at all, but at the time I did.

I don't know why I asked her to marry me. Probably because she lived a good length away from where I was living. I didn't have an automobile, and it was difficult to get transportation over to see her and get back to Long Beach where my apartment was, get up, get ready, and get to work and stuff like that. And I didn't like livin' alone. I never did. My friends I was batchin' with had all decided to go back to New Hampshire, and I was alone, and I didn't like bein' alone. Christ, I think I'da married anybody after a month of that. I just hated an empty house. I hated comin' in after work and there's nobody there.

We were over at her grandmother's out in the back yard in the swing one day, and I just said, "We love each other and we can't be together as much as we want to be together, so why don't we just consider gettin' married?" She thought it was a good idea. She got excited about it, probably kissed me and threw her arms around me and said she was hopin' I'd feel the same way . . . I don't know.

I had to send for permission to get married. I think you had to be twenty-one in California at the time. I know you did, 'cause I had to send for permission to get married. And they sent it, reluctantly sent permission. But they figured I'd go ahead and do it anyway, lie about my age or somethin'. They knew I was pretty headstrong and independent. They didn't know the girl at all. So they gave permission, begrudgingly. They didn't like the idea.

4

I got bumped off my job at Pacific Greyhound by somebody with more seniority. I went up to North American Aviation and

16

got some work. This was still 1954. I started out as a utility man in the machine shop, the lowest job you had. I'd just run around and clean other people's machines and clean the chips out of lathe beds, run stock for guys, and help 'em keep the machines running. That's when I became active in the union. We had what we called COPE, Committee on Political Education. I was active in that. I was always in the rallies. I was a speaker. When I was nineteen, I was speaking at rallies. I was chairman of the Downie Unit, which is the biggest unit in Local 887, a 22,000 voting-power unit. I was chairman when I was twenty, twenty-one years old. I had a column in the *Propeller,* which was a newspaper, our local newspaper.

Through the union I became a political power in the Long Beach area and southern California. Like our union alone had potential signup membership of 22,000 people. So you're influencin' a lot of votes. And judges and things out there are elected. Of course, mayors are elected everywhere. So they used to favor me, to get union backing. They'd call me at home on the phone, people who were lookin' for judgeships in that area.

A man who wanted to be judge or maybe mayor would call me at home and say he wanted to meet me. He'd tell me that he was a candidate and if there was some way he could make himself better known to us he'd appreciate it. He'd offer all kinds of favors—financial, parties for union officials, entertaining. Like he would support the education or retirement fund or he'd put some money in for the kids or he'd throw a party. The mayors used to always do that a lot. They would party an awful lot—luaus and barbecues—and they'd want you over to their house. And these were influential people. You see, we had something they wanted, and that was the vote.

This was the auto workers' union I was a member of. Leonard Woodcock was a friend of mine. Walter Reuther and I sat in planning teams before Reuther died. That lawyer who was with Kennedy when he got shot, he was a good friend of mine—Paul Schrade. In fact, Schrade was wounded. He was hit too. I was friends with all those people.

Well, with the connections I had and the things I had done, I figured I might be able to get into politics, and I decided that first I had to become a lawyer. So for that reason I enrolled in San Diego Junior College takin' classes at nights while workin'. I took introduction to psychology, English, and, of course, law. I figured that, because of my connections in labor, I could go pretty far in politics, at least as far as United States Senator from California. After that, who knows? It seems far-fetched now, sitting in prison and talkin' about somethin' like that, but it wasn't far-fetched at the time. It was entirely possible. I had good contacts. I didn't know Governor Brown personally, but he knew of my activities.

I was always doin' some silly thing, anyway, that kept me in the newspapers. I've always been able to do that for some reason. Like we sent a mile-long telegram to Washington when they canceled the Navajo Missile contracts and threw so many people in the streets. At North American Aviation they suffered quite a blow. The Navajo Missile cutback put thousands of people out of work, so I come up with the idea's of sendin' a mile-long telegram to Washington, protestin' the automatic cutoff with no warnin' and no replacement contracts, creatin' such a severe economic problem in the southern California area. And that got a lot of publicity, that telegram thing. It went out on the AP and the UPI. I had a lot of interviews and stuff. I was always doin' somethin' like that. I was in the newspapers. The *Los Angeles Times* didn't like us too much though. They was always a foe against labor.

So I had political aspirations. I had talent. I had contacts. I lacked education, but I was getting that and doing good at it. I was inspired and I had high aspirations. I could see clearly the way to go, and the plan was pretty well formulated. There was only one flaw in it, and that was my marriage.

You see, I had a problem. I don't know if the girl was lazy or didn't know how to be a housekeeper or what. She'd been raised by her grandmother and her grandmother didn't want her gettin' married. And she never required her to do any housework. I think it was a conscious effort on her grandmother's part so that she'd be undesirable to any man. I really believe that, because she just couldn't get herself organized. She wouldn't keep the house up. She was so bad with the housework that several landlords, though they liked me personally, had to come to me and say they just couldn't tolerate havin' their place be in such bad shape. She was just filthy, and we even had to change apartments because of that, several times.

I kept askin' her and talkin' with her and helpin' her and doin' everythin' I could to get her to come around, to get her to do the things that had to be done by a wife to support a guy that was in the things I was in and had the plans that I had going for myself.

It was a big problem. I knew it wouldn't help my political career any to be a divorcée. I didn't want a divorce. I was a faithful husband and a hard worker and a good provider. I wanted that marriage to be a success.

I couldn't have people in the home, though, and she never took care of the kids the way she should. I'd come home from a hard day's work, workin' overtime sometimes, and I'd be due at a special executive meetin' for the union up in Inglewood, near the airport on the Imperial Highway. I'd come home from work and have to cook supper. I'd have to wash the pans to cook the supper in, that's how bad it was.

I couldn't put up with it. I'd be workin' hard all the time, and she'd be readin' magazines, visitin' friends, and just goofin' off. I really tried and tried and tried. I got to be pretty much disgusted with her, and it was interferin' with our sex life.

I spent a lot of money for washers and dryers, everythin' for the house and for her. No matter what I got her, she didn't do a thing to improve. She had a problem. I think she probably needed a psychiatrist, but I didn't think along those lines back then. I didn't think of it. Maybe it would've straightened her out. I don't know. She sure needed somethin'.

5

We had this next-door neighbor. Her husband neglected her. He wouldn't even put money in the house for groceries. He'd go off bowlin', foolin' around, and everything. He wouldn't even care if there was any food in the house for his kids.

She started askin' if she could ride to the store with us and one thing and another, and her children played with my children, and every time I went out and fixed a barbecue she was always there. And she was a good-lookin' girl, but I wasn't thinkin' along those lines. For some reason I didn't. I don't know why, but that was the farthest thing from my mind.

I'd go over to her house, and I'd give her a kiss on the cheek or somethin', pat her on the butt, and I'd take off. I was always foolin' around with her like that, even in front of my wife, 'cause I wasn't tryin' to seduce her. But it was affecting her 'cause I didn't know she was being neglected as much as she was, in every way, sexually too.

One day I was foolin' around and not thinkin' a thing, and she says to me, "You know, you're not very fair."

And I says, "What do you mean?"

She says, "Well, you fool around, and you get me excited and you go off, you go home, and you're all right," she says, "but you leave me in pretty bad shape."

And then it came to mind. I failed with her, and I thought about it, and I told her I didn't realize I was botherin' her.

And she says, "Well, you do." She says, "You know, I think very much of you. You're important to me."

I told her I'd cut it out.

And she says, "Well, I didn't mean that, exactly—for you to stop."

So we started havin' sex. Like I'd take a night off college when I was supposed to be in college and I'd park the car around the corner and I'd go to her house next door, which is pretty close to home and seems kinda reckless. Part of it was maybe I was hopin' I'd get caught, 'cause I knew the marriage had to change or be lost anyway.

She didn't enjoy the sex with me at all. No, up to a point she did. She enjoyed the attention. She enjoyed the kissing and the foreplay. But the actual sexual act, the intercourse, she'd start to enjoy it and start to reach a orgasm and she'd stop, just before she should reach the fulfillment of the act. And that bugged me.

That really bugged me because in my marriage and before that with girls I was never one to satisfy myself and not be concerned about my partner in the sex act. So I asked her about it. I says, "What in the hell's the story?" I says, "I gotta know what's buggin' you."

She says, "Nothin'. Everthin's fine."

I wouldn't accept that. I knew somethin' was wrong. I kept after her. I told her, well, if we didn't find it out, if we didn't get it straightened out, if she refused to talk about it, we'd just quit doin' it, we'd just go back and be friends and not mess around no more. 'Cause if she wasn't gettin no more out of it than that, I felt like I was usin' her.

And she says, "All right, let me think about it." And next time she says, "I'll tell you. I'll try to."

So I went over and we talked about it. What had happened was like this. She was a virgin when she was married and so was her husband. They were both virgins. They had met at some Baptist Bible college, and they hadn't had no sex with anybody or together when they got married. Virgins, both virgins. And on their wedding night they went to a motel and started to have sex. And she was enjoyin' it and she got to breathin' hard and all kinds of stuff. And when she was gettin' excited and ready for her orgasm, he started laughin' at her. And every time after that, she just withheld and she wouldn't let herself go because of him makin' fun of her on their weddin' night. And I think that's what ruined his marriage right there. He ruined his marriage on his weddin' night.

So then I worked with her and I talked to her. I asked her, "You don't think I'd laugh at you?" I worked with her very much on that. And then she had an orgasm. She flipped right out. She thought that was really terrific. I was gentle with her and patient, and later on she thanked me for that, because she didn't think anyone else would have been able to make her enjoy life that much. She saw sex as a duty thing.

I really loved her and she loved me, and we talked sometime about gettin' together permanently, gettin' married. She was divorcin' her husband and I knew that my marriage was doomed, and so it was natural to think about it and to talk about it.

21

We knew we were in love and that it was a good thing. There were no lies. It was really nice. It was a beautiful relationship. It's one that I can look back on fondly, without any shame.

I don't know what happened. Oh, yes. We lost contact with each other. We didn't realize that we couldn't always be able to get hold of each other, and she had to go back to Arkansas, where her home was. And while she was gone, we didn't do any letter writing. She must have had a lot on her mind, too. I'm sure she did—problems and things. And I didn't know it, but she was planning on coming back to where I was, within a few months. But in the meantime I moved. I changed my residence. Neither her nor I knew a lot of people in the community. The neighbors I knew, but they were just casual acquaintances. There was no real close friendships, nobody that I would let know where I had moved to. And after I had moved away she did in fact come back and I was gone and she asked around, but nobody knew where I was. She couldn't find me. And one day in the supermarket I met her ex–father-in-law, and he asked me if I'd seen her. And I said no, and I said, "Why?"

And he says, "She was here last week. And she was very much upset, 'cause she wanted to see you."

And I said, "No, I didn't see her at all." And I says, "Do you know where she is now?"

He says, "No, I don't." He says, "I think she's gone back."

And I didn't know where she was, there in Arkansas. I knew she was in Little Rock, but I didn't know how to find her. I knew what her maiden name was, but I didn't know how the hell to find her. Little Rock's a big city. It drove me frantic for a while, and then I figured, well, maybe that's the way it should be, and I tried to make another go of the marriage, my own marriage.

Years later, I was travelin' through the country with my music, on a Grand Ole Opry show, and I was in Little Rock. It was pretty late at night. It was raining, and I went to a phone booth and went through all the names in the phone book which were the same as her maiden name. I made two or three calls, and maybe the third call I got her mother on the phone. And I asked her if she had a daughter named Cathy and she said, "Yes, I do. Why?" She got a little bit suspicious.

I says, "Look," I says, "we were friends in California," and I told her who I was.

And she knew my name. She said, "Oh, yes. I've heard her speak of you. She's talked with me about you."

And I says, "Is she there now?"

She says, "No. She's out. She's out bowling." And I asked how she was. She says, "She's fine," she had a boy friend and she was engaged to be married to this guy.

So I didn't even bother tryin' to see her. I just told her mother, I said, "You don't even have to tell her I called. I just wanted to know how she was, and if she's happy and engaged and stuff, I won't bother her."

She said, "Well, I'll certainly tell her you called."

I said, "Well, if you think that it's important, you do what you want."

She probably did. I didn't get sad over it then or afterwards. It didn't bother me, and I forgot it. I was a rip-roarin' musician then. That's when I was quite promiscuous, a tomcat.

6

I was pretty discouraged, disgusted with the marriage. I saw the things I'd worked for with the college and the union crumbling, and every day there was less chance of those developing any further. I got to drinkin', and messin' around with the pills, and mixin' them. Pills were legal then—amphetamines, barbiturates, Dexamyls, things like that. They used to get 'em at work. You know, like if a guy come in tired or if he'd been out partyin' over the weekend, and Monday and Tuesday he was feelin' rough and was runnin' equipment, like lathe operator or somethin', he'd just go down to the infirmary and the nurse would give you some bennies and perk you up. It used to be legal. Half the housewives in the country were drug addicts and didn't know it. They were all takin' weight-reducin' pills and takin' more than the doctor prescribed and gettin' their highs and really gettin' their kicks off gettin' their housework done. They were all junkies and didn't know it. I knew what they were. I knew what they could do, especially mixed with booze.

Everybody had 'em. They were legal. Maybe the Benzedrine weren't, but there were all kinds of people comin' around that would go to Tijuana, that was only a hundred miles away. Get 'em off police officers frequently. Some of your best contacts was police. I knew police at the college. They were in my classes. They got Benzedrine from busts. They were doin' it too.

I'd had it. The marriage had had it. The marriage had had it in its fifth year when I had the affair with the girl. Those last three years was just keepin' it together for the sake of the kids, which is just insane for people to do.

I hated my life with her—talking, talking, talking until I was blue in the face and then threatening not to be able to put up with it anymore and some day leaving her. She didn't believe that I would. Sometimes she'd say she'd try, and sometimes she did try, but it didn't last over four days. She'd say she was sorry nine million times. I got so sick of listenin' to her say she's sorry that I wouldn't listen to it from anybody else for years. I hate that word "I'm sorry." If you're sorry, don't do it. She was terrifically lazy and had been trained to be that way. She'd eat a lot of candy and read romance magazines and watch television. She didn't believe I'd leave her. Even when I threatened her, she didn't believe it. She was pampered and spoiled and I couldn't break her out of it. And the children, she neglected 'em, which angered me.

I got sick. I had my tonsils removed, adenoids, and a submucous resection. And infection set in. I hemorrhaged in recovery. I didn't know about it 'cause I was still unconscious. They told me afterwards that they almost lost me, that I almost died from the hemorrhaging. And afterwards it got infected. I was havin' a hell of a time with it, a lot of headaches, spending a lot of money on chiropractors and specialists and all kinds of things. Everyone had a different theory. I was gettin' shots for inflammation of the spine. They were tellin' me all kinds of stuff, and I never could figure out what in the hell was doin' it. They were migraines. I was havin' migraine headaches. It began to interfere

with my attendance on my job. I think maybe, too, it was trig-
gered by the stress and the strain of the work I was in, the hours
I was in, the hours I was puttin' in with the school, the union,
my employment, the problems at home. I was sufferin' migraine
headaches where it would blind me. I completed my last se-
mester of college with just a C where before I was the top student in my class. And it was foulin' up my attendance at work. I
couldn't hardly live with those migraines. They was actually kil-
lin' me. I thought I'd be better off dead.

I was tryin' to do too much too fast, I think, and I had the
home problems on top of it all. So, after eight years with the
company, they dismissed me for attendance. I knew it was
comin'. They have their rules and regulations, and you don't
keep comin' in late and miss days and still keep workin'. It's cut
and dried.

I had worked up to senior project planner in the planning department by this time. And I had the Minuteman Missile guid-
ance system as my project. In eight years' time that was quite an
advancement, one of the highest-paid jobs they had that was
nonsupervisory.

They called me to personnel and talked to me so that with the
rank that I held, it wouldn't be so impersonal. It's quite a thing
for them to fire somebody that's been workin' with them that
long and in that capacity. He just called me in and said that I'd
exhausted my sick leave and that, with my absenteeism like it
was, they couldn't use my services any longer and I was termi-
nated. And they was, you know, sorry, and I got my severance
pay. And they had their checks all made out and everything was
ready except the speech. And it wasn't much of a speech. And I
didn't care to hear it.

That was 1962. We had two boys at that time. Warren was
born in 1956, and Ben had been born in 1958. She was pregnant
with Cheryl at the time, and she had the baby that year.

I told my wife, I said, "I just got fired. It's gonna be hard for
us now, at least for a while." But it didn't bother her. She must
have been just assuming that I'd go out and get something
equally good or better. I don't think she realized the impact of
the thing. I don't know. She had this mental problem. She

didn't face these realities of life. I told her before that if she didn't straighten up, there'd be comin' a time when I'd leave. She didn't want me to to leave but she wasn't doing anything to make the marriage better either. She just wouldn't face reality and meet her responsibilities to the realities of life. She was passive, and even that can drive you to the point of distraction sometimes.

7

I had been playin' music part-time at union activities, functions, and one thing and another, and I just shifted into it full-time. You have to realize that the instrument I play, the steel guitar, is always in great demand wherever there's country music. So I didn't have any trouble findin' work and I was gettin' more successful every week. I met some professional musicians who were doin' a little recording and I got into that, so I got some recording experience in the studios. The Seattle World's Fair was on. Some guys come along who wanted to go up there, through Washington and Oregon, and do some barnstorming and see what they could pick up. So I decided to go with them 'cause I couldn't stand no more of my wife and I figured it might shock her into something and I'd come back in a month or so and see if it straightened her out.

I told her I was goin'. She didn't like the idea. She asked me not to go. I told her I was anyway. I didn't care what she'd say. I told her I'd be back and I told her if things didn't change I was gonna leave for good.

So we went out with no specific jobs in mind. It was just what they call barnstorming in the music business, picking up what you could along the way. We'd play at rodeos, country dances, pavilions, fairgrounds, lounges, all types of things. You'd just go in and try to sell it on the spot. We met a lot of people that wanted us to stay and, for one reason or another, we didn't like the town or the pay or the club or it didn't meet with our plans in some way and we didn't stay. We left. We ran into a lot of good opportunities and kept on going. Back then, of course, you were lucky if you made over twenty dollars a night. I've seen people work for a lot less than that, people you hear about now. Big stars and songwriters were havin' it pretty rough back in those years in California. Buck Owens himself was in Bakersfield and wasn't doin' all that good during those years.

But I got up into the Portland, Vancouver, Washington area by the interstate bridge there—Jansen Beach. We were havin' it a little bit rough but we were pickin' up some change too.

At one of clubs we was playin' at, we met an announcer or a disc jockey from radio station WCOB and he told us they needed help real bad and the station was hurtin' financially. The station had been really run down. It was owned by an alcoholic divorcée, and it was in pretty bad condition. The disc jockey I talked to sometimes would get to drinkin' applejack. He was supposed to be runnin' a Saturday night show and he'd go out in the back room nippin' on his applejack. He'd never get back into the control room. The record would just sit in there and swish all night long over the radio. It was in pretty bad shape.

They didn't have any money and we had a lot of time. Well, it worked out pretty good. All of the band became disc jockeys. And every guy in the band was kind of a kook, you know, each one in a different way. We got the station up to number three in the Portland area, from probably a fifteen position. We weren't gettin' paid but we were getting percentages on the sale of advertising, which picked up. Remington Rand and all these people started to show an interest in us because of our popularity. And it was the guys in the band that did it. We'd announce where we were playin' so that got crowds where we were playin' and made club owners more interested in having us.

I was living in Camus, Washington, for a while, and then I moved to Vancouver. Camus is where Jimmy Rodgers is from. He sang "Honeycomb." The guys got to likin' it up in that part of the country. It was good fishin'. We had lots of friends. We were popular. They wanted to settle in there and I thought it was a good idea too, and it would've been if we'd have stayed longer. We had a fella that wanted to book us, become a bookin' agent. He did in fact get us several jobs at Larson Air Force Base in Moses Lake, Washington—the Strategic Air Command. And they loved us up there.

8

My wife wanted to make another try at it. She promised that she would make a sincere effort, in discussions we had on the phone. So I relented. I went down and picked up her and the kids. I don't know. I wanted to be with the kids anyway. I've always loved the kids very much. I still do, always will.

And I thought things would be better, movin' out of the California area, gettin' her away from her family, and the influence there that wasn't good. And grandma. And the bill collectors were startin' to get pretty rough 'cause they weren't gettin' paid. I just couldn't keep up my bills after I lost my job, and I was obligated for quite a bit of money. They were houndin', houndin' all the time. I had quite a bit of furniture and stuff. I don't know what happened to it. I guess it was repossessed or stolen by so-called friends.

She didn't keep her word very long. It got bad up there too—dirty clothing lyin' all around, sink full of dirty dishes, meals not ready on time or, if it was, it was something that was just heated up out of a can. She'd've starved to death if I hid her can opener. She tried for a while, but I don't think she even knew how to keep house. I'd have to go to a laundromat. I'd have to do the wash with her or it wouldn't get done. She'd be willing to iron but she wouldn't do all the ironing. She'd iron me one shirt out of the pile and leave the rest for when I wanted it. It was ridiculous. And I'm not just bad-mouthin' her.

Well, finally I sent her packin'. I told her that I had enough of it and I was gonna send her back to LA and she could call and arrange to have her people pick her up—her parents—and I'd be gettin' in touch with her. I put her on the bus, her and the three kids, from Portland and sent her back to LA. I think she lived in a fantasy world. She always believed everthing was gonna be all right. She's unreal. I got on the bus and I kissed the kids. And I told her that maybe someday if she'd get straightened out, then maybe we'd have a chance but until she did there was no hope for us. I didn't say it in those words, not in public like that. I probably told her I hoped she'd get it together or somethin' like that. But she knew what I was talkin' about. She was sorry, she said, and she knew she could do better and she knew she was wrong. "I'm sorry" again. All that "I'm sorry" crap. She admitted she was wrong but she'd never do nothin' about it. And she'd never show any real feelin'. She was passive, very passive.

That was the break, as far as I was concerned. I knew then that I never wanted to see her again and maybe not the kids unless I could get away for a visit once in a while. And I really hit the bottle. Really. I wanted to die from drinkin'. I didn't have the courage, probably, or maybe I was too smart to just shoot myself or something. But I did fully intend to drink myself right into the ground. I tried to do it. It's a wonder I didn't become a alcoholic. It's a wonder I didn't get the disease. And I was on that kick for a long time, dependable but always half-drunk. It didn't hurt my show business any, 'cause the people I was around were like that too. Most of the time when I was in that condition it was party time, but you don't sustain that. There's moments of reckoning even when you're drunk, and then it's worse. I missed the kids real bad. And I was really depressed that the marriage didn't work and that everything I knew how to do at the time couldn't make it work. It came Christmas time and I really got bad off, bein' away from the kids for the first time. I wasn't makin' all that much money and, when I could, I'd send some money to the kids. I knew they weren't hurtin', 'cause her people weren't bad off. They weren't wealthy people, but they had steady jobs and more money than just to pay off bills and things. Her dad was a pretty nice guy, her step-dad, a religious person.

I went downhill from there, went to booze. That didn't help the band any. The other guys had problems too, personal problems, and we had conflicts. Some were unreliable. They'd show up late. They wouldn't get with it. So the band did break up. I stayed on with the radio station and I started tryin' to sell air time. I did make some sales.

9

On one of the trips up to Seattle I had met a singer who was very good. He had been a convict. I didn't know it at the time. It didn't matter. A lot of guys been in trouble with the law who was in music. David Conley or David Poole, he went by both names. I think his middle name was Conley, David Conley Poole. He was very good. He was entertaining up there on Pike Street, the Cavalhero Club, at the time. And I sat in and played with him. I'd never met him before but he liked my steel. Steels were hard to find, like I said before. And he wanted to work some stuff up. I said, "Sure. If you ever have anything let me know." Which I wouldn't've done if I'd've known all the hang-ups that guy had, all the problems he had.

He called me in Vancouver and said that he had an engagement in Colorado, playin' at this saloon in Colorado for room and board and I don't know if he said $125 or $150 a week. And he asked me if I would play steel for him at the place. I told him that I definitely would because things weren't too busy for me in Portland or Vancouver at that time.

So I did go down with him to that place in Colorado. It was up on the Western Slope, and it wasn't anything at all like he said it was gonna be. Like I had a room and it was in an old hotel, and it was pretty bad, run-down. The food wasn't that good. The bar had a little counter where they served people soup or somethin' like that and a sandwich once in a while. And that was pretty rough.

We worked in a saloon, the Dew Drop Saloon. That was the most popular place in town. With or without us it was popular, 'cause the lady owner played piano. She's been there for years and she could entertain and sing old songs and tell jokes. And people loved it, listenin' to her. If somebody'd gotten to her when she was younger and developed her talent, she probably could've been a star. She was very good and you could see that when she was younger she had to have been a very attractive girl. She was an attractive lady, but she just wasted away up there in that saloon. But she raised a family. She done what she wanted to do, I guess.

The money wasn't that much. The people were good to us but we didn't get anywhere near the money he told me we would get. We met a lot of people there, 'cause it was a kind of crossroads for trucking and the rodeo industry was through there all the time. We got to meet a lot of people.

It was a rough place, though. You had oil well roughnecks and you had sheepherders and you had the Basques and Mexican laborers and you had cowboys. It was a pretty rough place.

And Dave, he had a fireball temper, this guy. I can understand it, after having done time in prison myself, why a guy would get that way. I didn't understand it at the time. I thought he was the quickest-tempered guy I'd ever seen in my life. The owners knew Dave from before, he had worked for 'em before. They was always preachin' to him not to fight. They told him they wouldn't tolerate fightin' from the band.

There was a little squabble goin' on, over in one of the booths, and both of the owners were over there, talkin' to the people and tryin' to get it straightened out. And the owners had their backs to the bandstand. They weren't watchin' us. And Dave knew that.

And this guy come up to talk to me. And I was playin' the steel guitar and had my head down as I was playin'. And I can't talk and play very much, a little bit, but the steel requires a lot more concentration than some instruments. The guy was drunk and he was pretty obnoxious and he was a wise guy. I said, "I can't talk. See that guy." And I kept playin'. He put his hands across my strings, and the minute you do that they deaden right out. I gave his hand a shove and kept playin' 'cause I didn't want to throw the rest of the band off, we had people dancin'. Like I said, the guy was obnoxious. He had an obnoxious personality, overbearing. He thought we was supposed to just stop everything and listen to him, I guess. And we had the place full of people. So I told him, I says, "Hey, get away from me."

He went up to Dave and he said, "Hey."

Dave said, "What?" I was playin'. Dave had stopped singin'. I was playin' the instrumental part of the song.

The guy says, "You know something, your steel player is a son of a bitch." Something like that. He called me a name.

Dave says, "I can't hear you. Come here. He says, "What's the matter?" The guy said it again, and Dave flattened him, knocked him clean across the dance floor and into a booth. He just cracked him without sayin' a word, split his mouth open. He was always in fights, Dave was. But it wasn't hard to do around there, I'll tell ya. It was pretty rough. His girl was workin' there as a waitress, and he'd bop guys that would get wise with her.

Then it got to be off season or somethin', so the owners told us they had to cut down on the nights. We stopped playin' full time, went to two or three nights a week, and I had to have other income, so I went to work in a wool shed and in a radio station, grabbin' anything I could. The radio station didn't pay much. Most radio stations don't pay much unless they're in the top forty and you're a high-powered deejay with a big rap and a big followin'. And I was drivin' a truck up to the oil fields, old truck, wasn't even fit to be on the road, didn't have good brakes and stuff, and I was drivin' on them mountain passes. And I worked as a cowboy on a ranch for a year. And I worked for a man named Mr. McKee, heating and refrigeration, real nice fellow, beautiful guy, and his whole family was nice.

10

All the time, it seems, there was this force inside makin' me look for religion.

I'd been searchin' for a religion from the time probably I was around fourteen years old. I just had somethin' inside of me makin' me do it. I don't know why I did it. My parents weren't religious and never attended any church, but a friend of mine, Jimmy Wilson, and I attended vacation Bible school of the Seventh-Day Adventist Church when we were kids. We learned crafts, things about the Bible, things about Christ. It was fun, we enjoyed it, and we had an outing at the end of Bible school, up in Milton.

I was always lookin'. Then one time we done Christmas carols and we went up and rung the bells at the Methodist church. And my grandmother was very religious too. She'd sing religious songs when she was an old lady. I can remember her holdin' me on her lap and rockin' me, singin' about Jesus and heaven and stuff like that.

I kept lookin' for somethin' that was truthful. I was lookin' for a church where its full programs and all of its teachings were acceptable to me. I couldn't find it. When I found one little thing that I felt was an untruth or was bein' taught in a manner that was contrary to the example of Christ, then it was all gone. I wanted the whole thing, and I knew that there had to be somethin' somewhere that was completely true, or what I believed and felt was completely true.

Sometimes I'd read the scriptures and I'd read that God is not the author of confusion. But it seemed like I saw an awful lot of confusion in all the religions I had any experience with. By that I mean lack of coordination, jealousies between the people, not going anywhere. You know, where do they come from? where are they going? and why are they here? Nobody answered those questions. There was an exceeding amount of confusion, a lot of pretending. In the mission there was people pretending to speak in tongues. It was just an act. They'd shout and squirm and fall down, and it was all a show. I couldn't stand that.

I had known this man at work, in California, that was a Mormon. He didn't preach to me, because I didn't ask for it. He'd only answer questions when I'd ask him. He didn't force it on me. And he was one of the nicest guys I ever met. Then I met some more Mormons when I started playin' music in Colorado. Joanne, she was a Mormon. She was married to the son of the people that owned that Dew Drop Saloon where I played, and she was a very, very good singer, a terrific singer, and a very attractive woman. But she didn't influence me, because she wasn't living her religion and she didn't know much about it. She just happened to be born into it. Maybe on Easter or somethin' she'd dress her kids up and take 'em to the church service. She didn't practice family home evening, which is Mondays, when Mormons stay home together and be together as a family, and other important things. She just didn't know about it or she just let it go.

I went to one of the Mormon churches in Colorado and I almost turned away from it completely because one of the members there, one of the female members, got up and was talkin' in one of the meetings. And she was severely chastising the young priests for their conduct, datin' girls that weren't Mormons and things like that. I didn't understand it and I didn't like her mouthin' off. I almost never did go back, but the bishop in that area and I had a talk about it. You see, I was workin' at the gas station then, and the bishop of the church there and I had a discussion. I told him I didn't approve of the things I'd heard, and I says, "If that's the way it is, I'm not goin' back, 'cause these are the things I've found fault with in other religions."

He said, "Well, whether she is right or wrong, or whether anybody you ever meet is right or wrong, it would be a mistake for you to judge the entire Church by the activities of one person. They could very well be wrong. But that doesn't mean they have Church approval. If they're wrong, the Church doesn't approve." He says, "I recommend you just look at the doctrine of the Church, the doctrine and covenants, and learn a little more about it and then decide for yourself." He was a real terrific guy and he made a lot of sense to me. He says, "I'm concerned about you and I want you to make the right decision and make it intelligently." He says, "I don't want to pressure you, but, all through your experience with it, as long as you do stay with it, don't judge the Church by me and don't judge it by any other one person." He says, "Just look at the whole thing. I think you'll see the truth in it, like I did."

I thought that was wisdom and I responded to it. And I did, in fact, after a while, embrace the faith as what I had been lookin'

for and became baptized again in the Mormon faith. But I didn't
follow through on it, and that's partly my fault. I think it was
also partly the fault of whoever was supposed to be my home
teachers. They were slack, and they didn't come out and talk to
me at times when I should've been talked to. I was kind of mis-
guided and I fell away. Although I was a Mormon and I believed
in it, I kept gettin' further and further away from it. But I knew it
was right.

11

Somehow my wife had found out where I was, or maybe I called
there. I don't recall clearly how that went. Maybe I called there
to see how the kids were. I sent some money from there. I talked
to her on the phone. She wanted to know if I was comin' back. I
said I never was comin' back. And she said she didn't see any
sense in our stayin' married, and she was goin' to get a divorce.
I said, "Good, you won't get no trouble from me." I said, "You
don't even have to tell 'em where I am. You can tell 'em you
don't even know where I'm at, and that'll make it all the easier
for you. I won't contest the divorce." I thought at that time that
the kids belonged with their mother, that all children did, which
is a fallacy. But I believed it at the time. 'Cause there's nothin'
worse than a divorcée about six months later. I don't care who
they are. If they're foolin' around, if they're goin' out to to the
night clubs and things like that, it's livin' hell for them kids. And
I'm not sayin' that all women are like that, but if they're goin'
out to the bars and goin' to dances and drinkin' and datin' different guys, it don't take long for it to be right in the house with
the kids. And the kids are affected by it.

Well, she said she was gettin' a divorce, and I said that's
good, that's exactly what I wanted. I said, "You might as well,
'cause you're not seein' me ever again."

And she discussed maybe makin' it work. She said she could
make it work now, she didn't take me serious before but she

realized then I was serious. She said, "Will you give me another chance?"

And I said, "No. I'm done with it."

12

I got a call from New Jersey, of all places. It was the band that I'd gone to Oregon and Washington with. They had regrouped and got themselves way over in the East Coast somewhere. Charlie Beau James of the Tune Kings, he was the singer of the band. He said he had a good deal, a lot of work, backin' some stars. He had a steady engagement at one club which was pretty nice at Penns Grove, New Jersey. My brother had come to visit me and he decided to stay. He was drummin' with me at the time, and Charlie wanted me and my brother to come out there to New Jersey from Colorado. It seems like this was the wintertime 'cause we ran into some snow and stuff leavin' there. I think it must have been December. I figured this was a good chance to get back to the East Coast and get close to my family. It was not that far from New Jersey to New Hampshire. I figured I'd get home once in a while.

Now, Joanne had broke up with her husband Jack. They had a very stormy marriage. There was a lot of fighting and trouble in their marriage but I didn't get involved. I like 'em both. I was a friend of both and I wouldn't take sides. I stayed out of their personal business, and I didn't have any designs on Joanne either at the time. I knew that she was a very good-looking girl and very talented, but I was not tryin' to have an affair with her or mess around. I don't think she did mess around when they were married. I've seen her with him and without him, and she was pretty loyal and faithful.

But she had broken up with him, and they were headed for divorce. They had been separated many times, and she'd gone home to her parents in Steamboat, Colorado. And I thought, well, she wasn't doin' anything and she was havin' trouble financially. On the way through, I stopped and asked her if she'd like to go to the East Coast. I told her she could go with us, that we were going and we was goin' to reorganize the band with Charlie Beau James and the Tune Kings, and I was goin' to be the band leader. I told her if there wasn't work right then, I'd make sure she didn't go hungry and we'd soon get work that would include a girl singer. I wanted a girl singer in the band and she was the best I'd heard. She couldn't make up her mind right then. She said finally she didn't think she would go.

So I went back to New Jersey and got things organized pretty well with the band, got it organized and got a real good band goin'. I'd been there maybe a month and I got a call from Joanne. She wanted to know if there was an opening. I said, "There always was."

She wanted to know if Jack could come. I don't know what the reason was why she wanted him to come along, whether it was for security or she felt sorry for him and wanted to get him a start in the business or still had feelings for him. I didn't have any idea. I said, "I don't have work for another fellow in the band." I told her the only thing we could put on was a girl singer and even then the owner didn't want that.

The owner didn't want us to add any more pieces to the band. He was satisfied with the crowd he was drawing. He even questioned why I wanted a girl. But I had plans for the future that didn't include him. I wanted the band to become real good and get a bookin' agent and start dressin' up good and become professional and start makin' some serious money. And to do all that I had to have a girl singer and I wanted Joanne. She was the only one I knew, anyway, and she was good, like I said.

Finally I told her to come along and bring Jack and we'd make out somehow. We'd pool our resources. We might not be eatin' too well but we'd make it. And if they wanted to come under those terms where you work when we work and you don't work when we don't work and it's rough for a while, then that was fine with me.

And she said, "That's all right. I understand."

He understood too. I talked with him. I told him I didn't want no trouble, no family trouble. He was insanely jealous of her. I says, "When we're on stage, it's professional. You keep your private matters at home. You won't be fightin' in the clubs, or one of you will be gone. I think it'll be you, 'cause she's more valuable to the band than you are." I says, "I ain't sayin' that to hurt your ego. You're a good musician and all that. But what we need is a girl singer, and there isn't any better than her and you know that." I says, "I don't mind your comin' along if you be a real asset. But if there's any trouble, you go. That's it. We want it understood from the start."

He says, "Okay, man, I won't be no problem." 'Cause we were pretty close friends too, he and I. We'd gone through some scrapes together in Colorado. A guy tried to strangle him one night and I nailed the guy, slapped him up side of the head. Another time there was some steelworkers in town and they come up there lookin' for trouble and they were messin' around, kickin' a wastebasket, some foolish thing. He said, "Hey, don't do that." It was his mother's and father's club.

They said, "What business is it of yours?"

And he said, "Well, my people own the club. I'm gonna own it some day and, besides that, I just don't want you doin' that." Well, one guy grabbed him from behind, another one pinned his arm, and the third one was goin' to do a hell of a job on him. Before he could get his swing back and let it fly, I was on him, thumpin' him pretty good. He didn't even know I was there. I knocked him pretty silly. It was a pretty good battle. We kicked the three of 'em out of the club, he and I, and we strutted around about that, 'cause they were pretty good-sized guys and we whipped 'em proper. So we were pretty close for those reasons. We had these ties, and we were friends. He thought quite a bit of me, and he liked the way I played music.

The band got going good up there. I met this girl. She was a cute girl. She lived in the set of apartments upstairs from where the band was when I drove in to New Jersey. I stayed with them at first—the band—downstairs, and we were batchin', you know, livin' as bachelors. There was girls around, and my brother was there; and he's kind of nutty anyway. He loves a good time. Most musicians do, especially when they're loose like that, and we didn't have no ties. Not a one of us had a girl with us there at the time, so not a one of us were tied down or responsible so we were raisin' a lot of hell and partyin' and playin' our music and gettin' our songs down. The girls liked that too, and there was girls around. They weren't married.

I met this girl upstairs, like I said, and she seemed to take a likin' to me. We'd rap a lot. She was pregnant. She was showin'. She was maybe four or five months pregnant. She had a little belly on her, but she was a good-looking girl, very cute, attractive, and had one hell of a personality. But I didn't want a girl friend at the time.

She she got me up there and cooked the dinners, and asked me to stay over one night if I wanted to. So I went to bed with her. She always wanted me to tell her I loved her. I told her I wouldn't. She said, "Well, even if you don't mean it, just say it."

I said, "I don't know where you're comin' from. I don't mess around with crap like that. If I say it, I usually mean it."

She got to likin' me very much, too much, and I wasn't goin' for that. Here she is, pregnant by somebody else, and I didn't know who. She didn't tell me and I didn't question her. I didn't figure it was any of my business. It would've been if there was gonna be any permanent relationship, but I told her there was nothin' permanent, I was just passin' through. If she wanted to have a good time, fine.

She treated me ten times better in the little time I knew her than all the time I had known my wife. She took care of my clothes for me . . . She liked it. She was playin' house or somethin', I don't know what she was doin'.

Actually she was a syndicate girl from Florida and she got pregnant from the head kingpin down there. She was actually more than a hooker to them, she procured other girls. I didn't know all these things until later on.

Instantly she didn't like Joanne. She was very jealous because Joanne would consult with me about clothing, about songs, about what was happenin' with the band, was she doin' all right. . . . Joanne and I were very close friends for years, ever since I met her in Colorado. We were very close friends. Joanne didn't think much of her, either, and Joanne thought that was my baby, that I got her pregnant, but she didn't say nothin'.

13

I got the band hooked up with a booking agency in Philadelphia. It was a big agency, known all over the world. We had a good thing goin'. We got the band booked into Jacksonville, North Carolina, the first band to play down there on the strip, near Camp Lejeune, and we moved down there. The club wasn't open yet, and we got situated. They built a special club for us to open.

Things went good down there, except in Jacksonville there are probably 10,000 marines and 6 women. That's really bad. Joanne was popular, they loved her. We were an instant success, and we were makin' good money and havin' offers from all over the place, to go to Toronto, Canada, here, there. We were actually booked to go to the Golden Nugget in Las Vegas for two weeks' option in September. We were right near the top. There wasn't a band in the country that could touch us, replace us, for less than $1,500 a night. Like when our booking agent had us come up to Philadelphia to do publicity photographs, they had a hell of a time replacin' us. In fact, they couldn't. Their business fell off till we got back. And the owner was screamin'.

We was stuck there a long time, too, beyond our contract date. We got onto our booker about that. It was because the owner had an in with him. The bookin' agent was hirin' a lot of talent for the owner's other clubs, and as a favor to him our booking agent was leaving us stuck down there. Every time our option came up, we didn't want to renew but the owners wanted to renew, even at the increased percentage. So our money kept goin' up but we kept bein' stuck in this one place. You know, it's hot down there. It was bad. And Jack was havin' trouble now with Joanne. He was very, very jealous and he was havin' trouble keepin' it off the stage. I used to counsel him, "Look, you're divorced. You can't run her life for her."

He says, "Well, I can't stand it."

I says, "Well, you're gonna have to leave, then."

She asked me what she should do. I said, "Well, I don't think you ought to date people in front of him. If you're gonna date, you ought to be sensible about it and make dates when the band's not active. Go to some other place, go to a resort, go to Myrtle Beach. Keep your dates out of town, and don't flaunt it in front of him." I said, "He can't live with that. You've been man and wife."

She says, "Well, I'm not goin' back with him." She says, "I don't care about these other guys. I'm not doin' anything with them. I'm not doin' anything wrong." She says, "But I'm not goin' to turn a guy down if he wants to take me out to supper." She says, "You don't mind, do you? I'm not doin' anything wrong. And as far as he's concerned, he's got no say over me."

So I says, "You're right. He doesn't."

She said she was gonna enjoy her social life. If somebody decent, a friend, wanted to take her out to dinner, she'd go. And Jack couldn't stand that.

One night I was layin' in my room in the hotel. I was havin' headaches again during that time too. For some reason they were comin' on me pretty bad. I don't know, I was workin' hard with the band, developin' it. And one of the guys, the band leader, was poppin' a lot of pills and drinkin' a lot. He was gettin' flaky. I was tryin' to keep him in line, 'cause we had a good thing goin'. We already had the engagement signed for the Golden Nugget, which is probably one of the biggest shows you can play in country music. And the pay was good. Canada was showin' an interest in us, some of the big clubs up there, the Hotel Edison in Toronto and places like that. We was talkin' about big money now, one-nighters and flyin' around. We were just gettin' into the rewards of all the years of effort we'd put in, all of us. But things weren't really as solid with the guys as they should be. I guess it's always that way when you get five or six different personalities involved and that many different families sometimes.

I was layin' in my bed and I heard this kind of scratchin', bumpin', on my door to my room. I opened the door and there was Jack, covered with blood from his head to his toes. He was in his underwear and he'd gashed his arms open, almost to the bone it looked to me. I've seen that since then, here in the prison, but that was the first time I'd seen anything like that. It turned me off. In a way I hated him right then. The friendship was gone. I was concerned about his life. I didn't want the publicity for the band. There had been some trouble in town with other bands. A girl had died mysteriously in a bathtub. A radio supposedly fell and electrocuted her. She was supposed to be performin' abortions on other girls, and there was all kinds of damn stuff goin' on in that town. We didn't need that kind of publicity. It was a rotten town, really. You can guess it would be, with a military base and all, entertainers and everybody tryin' to get the guys for their money. The marines, they were suckers. They were far away from home, just through boot camp. I've seen 'em go out and buy things on credit and turn around and sell it for a third or even less at the hock shop. You could buy brand-new stereos, tape decks, TV's, anything you want. And guys would do anything for ten or twenty bucks a couple weeks after pay day. It's pretty bad.

Well, Jack was in bad shape. He was in real bad shape. He had lost a lot of blood. And he says, "Help me," you know.

So I helped him. I did have some medicines that I thought would help him. He should have been sewed up, but he wouldn't go to the doctor. I said, "We gotta find a doctor. We'll give him a different name or any damn thing to keep you out of it, to keep the band out of it. If the doctor has to have that information, we'll give him a phony name. But you gotta see a doctor. That has to be sewed up." He was wide open, both arms.

He wasn't bleedin' that much. It had clotted up. I guess he didn't get in an artery. He probably got some veins and stuff, but he didn't get in an artery and he was clottin' up.

I got to his room, and his bathroom was covered with blood, from the ceiling to the floor and all the walls. It was a really gory mess. I cleaned that all up, so the people in the hotel comin' in the next day deliverin' linens and things wouldn't find it. He refused, absolutely refused, to go to the doctor. I said, "You need stitches."

He said, "I don't care."

I said, "You're gonna have terrible scars if you don't get it stitched up." I says, "You might even need blood. You're white." I discussed it with him. He wouldn't go. The most he would do was let me tend to it, and I put some of the powder that I had into it, probably Terramycin or some antibiotic powder. And I wrapped him.

After that was all done, I talked with him for a while. He said he couldn't stand it no longer, he was gonna leave. I said, "You might just as well. I can't put up with this." I says, "We can't have it, you're gonna ruin the band." I says, "We've got big things goin'."

He says, "I know it." He says, "I'm just not fit to stay with the band. I can't take the things that are goin' on, the pressure that's on me." He asked me if I could loan him some money, one thing and another. So I got him on his way.

And I didn't know it, but Joanne was interested in me. She had become interested in me, I guess, because of the counselin' I was givin' her and the things I was doin' for the band. I don't know what it was, 'cause I don't fancy myself any Don Juan. I know she loved my guitar playin', and I think she respected the way I was always business minded and keepin' things together and counselin' people and gettin' on my brother's butt when he'd get to drinkin' too much. I was really serious then, and things were really goin' together right.

So she asked my brother what was wrong with me. She dropped hints and I didn't pick up on 'em, that she was interested. And he talked to me about it. I said, "You're crazy."

He said, "I'm not either. She don't look at nobody else but you."

Everybody came to my room before the shows 'cause the costumes would be there, one thing and another, and she'd start comin' in when two or three of us were dressin' up for the night. We'd be dressed in our costumes, and she'd come in and ask me to tie her neckerchief or some phony kind of crap. And I thought she was really serious, that she had to have me do it. I didn't think nothin' of it. She kept doin' little things. She kept leanin' on me. Everytime I'd go to eat somewhere, she'd ask if she could go. She started to be pallin' around with me all the time, and we began an affair.

Well, finally the band broke up. In spite of all our plans, in spite of the fact that we had a date to play at the Golden Nugget in Las Vegas, I couldn't keep us together. The people just had too many problems to stick with anythin' no matter how much they put into it, and that thing with Jack didn't help. We were plannin' to go to Las Vegas in September, and the band broke up in July or maybe August.

I picked up some local musicians, some guys in the service that were pretty good. We didn't have the quality of the band that I came there with, and the agent was concerned because he was makin' money with us and he had a lot of plans for the future, like the Golden Nugget. So he was puttin' pressure on me to keep things organized and replace the guys that left, the best I could. And Joanne was the main attraction anyway, and the steel guitar itself. So we had the most important parts of the group. He wanted me to build around it, and I tried to do it some way but I wasn't havin' much success.

Joanne and I decided to get out. It wasn't too easy. We had tried to before, but the owner wouldn't let us. He said, "I'll claim the instruments belong to me or I'll plant dope in your car and have you stopped on the state border, if you try to leave." He knew that his business would go way down if we left, and he'd do anything to keep us there. I had heard that that's the way it is with some of these clubs. I knew that it was like this in Chicago. The people I met in California, strippers and musicians and bartenders, had warned me about Chicago. They told me that you can't get out of there when you want to, especially if you're good. That's why I never went there, even though the band had a lot of chances to play Chicago.

I told the owner we were willing to settle down in the area. He said, "Good." He was happy then.

I said, "The only thing is that we gotta go pick up the kids, Joanne's kids who are back in Colorado, and we'd need our pay plus a couple of hundred dollars." And I got the fool to give it to me. We took off and never came back.

He got a little bit suspicious when we took our instruments with us. He asked, "Why are you takin' your instruments if you're comin' back?"

I said, "Well, we are professionals now, and we got a lot of friends that we've played with in the past, and we're gonna see them again. They're not gonna let us get away without playin'."

He says, "All right." Then he asks, "Are you sure you're comin' back?"

I says, "Oh, yeah, we're comin' back." He didn't think we were comin' back. I says, "I'm definitely comin' back. I can see this is a place where I can definitely make some money."

He says, "Look. I'll give you the house, everything." The guy was really serious. He was turnin' over a big business there. He saw too that when we weren't there, like when we went to Philadelphia for the photographs, he hurt. There was a lot of competition around there. And when we weren't there, people went other places.

So that's how I got out of that. I tricked him.

14

I was with Joanne at that time, and we went back and forth between Colorado and New Hampshire for a while. It seems like in those few years' time I drove across the United States fifty times.

First we went to Colorado and we picked up the kids, Joanne's kids, and we stayed there for a while. Then we went to my home in New Hampshire and, after a while, back to Colorado. I'd get any job I could. I was a gas station attendant. I also worked as a cook. But the main thing was to be playin'. The other things was just temporary.

When we were in New Hampshire, Joanne and I got married.

It wasn't my idea and I didn't care at that time. But she said, "I don't feel right about us this way." And she says, "If you don't mind, would it be all right with you if we get married?" She said she felt the relationship warranted us gettin' married. I went along with it. Later I found out I was still married to the first one. Not that I cared. At that time I wouldn't have cared. I loved Joanne very much, but it didn't matter to me if we got married.

Well, we came back to Colorado for a visit. I was tryin' to decide what to do. I had a little money saved up and I figured we had a lot goin' for us. I was fairly talented on the steel, and I thought she had everything that was required to become a star. I still do. She's that good. And I asked her what she thought about goin' to Nashville.

She says, "Do you think we'd make it?"

I said, "Look, I'm not afraid of work. I don't mind puttin' up the guitar for a while and doin' other things until we do make it." I says, "You know I think you're good enough. And I think that's the only place to go and really rough it out and find out if we can make it."

She says, "All right. Anything you want to do." She says, "I love you, and I trust you. And you've always done right for me." She had a lot of faith in me and in herself. She knew she was pretty good. She was more than that, she was fantastic.

So we went to Nashville, and we left the kids in Colorado until we made some money and got set up. It's not that easy to break in, I don't care how good you are. There's cliques in every locality, and it takes a while to get known. You gotta be good, but you gotta be more than that. You gotta be dependable, for one thing. And it takes a while for people to find that out. Your name has to get around. And you have to be accepted. It doesn't matter just how good you are.

I went down there, and I started goin' around to the clubs where the entertainers gathered. She went with me frequently. And I met a lot of people. I made a lot of contacts. She did too. We picked up part-time work, pushin' records, tryin' to sell 'em. Some guy would come in with a song or something, and if I liked it I tried to sell it to some star. And I'd get a percentage. I got streetwise to Nashville. I'd meet people in a bar or hangin' around an agency or rappin' in a restaurant. Everybody thought you was a star down there, you know. If you sat around with a pair of jeans on and a pair of boots and denim shirt or somethin', people comin' to town would look you over and see if they'd seen you before.

And I got work right away on the steel guitar. Like I toured with some names. I toured Florida with the Cousin Wilbur show. And they all wanted autographs. They even wanted the bus diver's autograph. Florida's a hell of a state to play in. They're the most enthusiastic fans of any place in the United States. I went over there with Mel Tillis, too. We went to Orlando. Joanne went on that one. She didn't go on all of them but she went on some. Like Cousin Wilbur and his wife went on tour, she'd stay at their house, babysit their kids. That would save us money too. I'd be on the road, livin' with the band, and she'd be livin' at their house, takin' care of their kids. We had it pretty good. I met Holland Howard, the songwriter, and went over to his studio. He offered to let us use his studio any time we wanted to cut demo tapes and things. Joanne did in fact sing some songs. I went around everywhere. I went to Pappy Dailey. I went to the Schwoburn brothers. Everybody. I didn't know such a thing as a closed door or a stranger. I talked with everybody.

We knew a lot of people, a lot of stars down there. We knew 'em personally and some of 'em were friends. We went to places where we knew we would meet these people and we'd associate with them for that prime purpose, to get into the business.

We were sittin' talkin' one night, and a big girl singer, big today, I'll call her Ginny Johns, was at the table. Joanne knew that she had children, and Ginny had just come back from a trip to Germany. There were a lot of air bases and military installations there, and she was telling her experiences. Joanne asked her what it was like to be on the road like that and goin' all around the world and leavin' the kids home. And that should have been a danger signal to me there, you know.

Ginny really laid it on, that it was so terrible and she couldn't hardly stand it sometimes, that she was thinkin' of quittin', lyin' through her teeth. She was deliberately discouragin' Joanne 'cause she knew Joanne was really good, maybe better than her.

That's the kind of thing that goes on in that business. I've seen record companies that will take a singer, a new singer, and sign a contract with him and put him on the shelf to protect one of their stars. It's a vicious business. You gotta know what you're doin' or you can get hurt. Well, Ginny Johns told how bad it was bein' away from the kids, that she was gonna quit, it was so bad. She ain't quit yet.

I was workin' at Western Auto, and John Owens at Hubert Long called me up. He says, "I got some good news for you."

I says, "What's that?"

He says, "Well, you were in here the other day talkin' about work." He says, "The fair conventions are comin' up. We've decided to put out 15,000 handbills on you and Joanne and sell you in a package with some of our other artists."

I says, "Well, what do we have to do?"

He says, "You don't have to do nothin'. You just have to get ready to go. When the fair season starts, you'll be all over the United States and parts of Canada." He says, "All the bookings will be done ahead of time and we'll just give you the dates, your itinerary, and you'll just have to be there." He says, "You'll be workin' with big stars. You'll be workin' with other people you don't know. You'll be part of our package, our fair package." He says, "I want you and her to come down, sign the contracts."

I says, "Well, what kind of money are we talkin' about?"

He says, "We'll guarantee you $150 a show for the two of you. That's not very big money," he says, "but I guarantee you twenty-two days a month work, at $150 a day. And that's a guarantee on the contract. If you don't work, you get paid anyway." That is cheap, that's the lowest pay in Nashville. But Joanne and I signed the contracts.

15

We were booked into the Boca Chica Naval Air Station, Joanne and I was, for $1,800 for New Year's Eve. We had to agree to stay there for two weeks, playin' four nights a week. That's eight nights, for an additional, I think, $2,500. It came to over $6,000 for New Year's Eve and eight more nights. I myself booked that in December. I had met the manager on one of the Florida tours. The guy was real happy to get us. I had my musicians picked out to go and Joanne was gonna be the headliner. I had already talked about promotin' Joanne, and she was part Cherokee anyway. We was gonna put on a gimmick and have her as an Indian princess. Morningstar was gonna be her name, and the band was gonna dress all in frontiersman outfits. She was gonna come out in white buckskin with an Indian head-band. It would've sold. This was back in 1964 or '65, and it would have been a front-runner to all this Indian movement stuff. The timing was perfect for it. There was no way she could've helped but become a superstar. It would've happened.

Joanne wanted to go home for Christmas. She got lonesome for the kids and asked to go back. On the way the car broke down. It blew up. So we both went back by bus, Greyhound. Her people were in Wyoming then, not Colorado. The kids were up there with the grandparents. Well, she got back there and she cried and cried and cried when she saw the kids and hugged them.

It was that night, after she saw the kids and the kids were in bed, that she tells me, "I'm not goin' back. I know this'll disappoint you, but I'm gonna quit show business. The kids are more important to me than that."

It took me kind of by surprise. It confused me. I said, "Why?"

She said, "I can't be the kind of mother I want to be and still be in show business."

I said, "I'm sure we can work somethin' out. I know we can make the kids more a part of our life than they have been." I said, "What you're sayin' doesn't make sense. How can you give up everything you've always wanted, all of a sudden like this?" I said, "Here's somethin' you've wanted all your life and you're going to turn your back on it right at the last minute. I can't believe it. I refuse to believe it. It's what you want. It's definitely what you've wanted, all your life."

She said, "I've got to make some sacrifices for my kids. I'm serious about it."

I didn't know if she'd change her mind or not. I sure as hell didn't feel like goin' back to Nashville by myself, with all our plans ruined. I said to her, "I'll stay here too. How can I go back by myself? I'll pick up some kind of work, just like I've always done. I'll stay here with you and the kids, take care of you. It'll give us time to think things out."

She said she didn't want me to. She said, "You tried to quit before and it didn't work." She was right, I had tried to quit music when her and I settled a little bit in New Hampshire, but I came back to it before long. She said, "It's in your blood. You can't quit it, not because of me." She said, "I know you'll be miserable. You'll be so miserable it'll destroy us anyway."

So I had no choice but to go back to Nashville. I had to go back there by myself. I thought she needed time to think. I'd give her the time and in the meantime talk to her on the phone, get her to be more rational. I figured that this would be a setback for our plans but it wasn't necessarily the end of 'em. She had the talent and nothin' would change that. So I took the bus back to Nashville.

I called the people in Florida where we was supposed to appear at New Year's Eve, and I told 'em that we weren't gonna make it. I told 'em what had happened. I said she had children from a previous marriage, she went back for Christmas vacation, and she had let me know that she wasn't gonna appear. They wanted me to find some other girl and call her Joanne because they had already put the posters up and all that stuff. I said, "I can't do that. I don't know any girl singers here in Nashville." There was one girl who sang bass, but she couldn't front the band. And I had some connections but I didn't have that many. I said, "All the people I know are working, and they all have prior obligations."

He says, "Jesus." He says, "Well, the job's open. What I'll have to do is put in some local talent. But right up to New Year's Eve itself, if you can get something together, fly in. Make the show."

I never did it. I couldn't get anythin' together. And I played that New Year's in Marietta, Georgia, with another band, playin' steel.

Then I went to Hubert Long and told 'em what happened and asked 'em what they suggested. They had already printed up all the material on us and stuff, but they said, "That's not so important. It's a minor thing. It happens. Is there any chance of talkin' her into returnin'?"

I said, "There's always that chance. She loves the business, and she knows she's good."

They said, "Try to do that and in the meantime try to build somethin' else."

I told 'em I would. I had established good relationships with that agency, and they're one of the biggest in country business, the Hubert Long talent agency. Some of the biggest stars are with them. John Owens was a good friend of mine, and he was their talent coordinator and director. A hell of a nice guy.

I was doin' a lot of talkin' to Joanne on the phone, but she said, "It's rough and we're not makin' it any easier on each other by keepin' in contact." She said she definitely made her mind up and she thought we just better go our separate ways and we had reached the fork in the road. I saw it that way, too, something that neither one of us actually wanted as far as her and I bein' together. It just couldn't be. We reached the place where I didn't fit in her life and she no longer fit in mine. It was her choosing and I had to respect it. It would've been easier for me to understand it if she had met someone else or somethin' like that. I could've got angry at somethin' like that. But I couldn't get angry at what happened. All I could do was be hurt.

16

We had a song stolen off us that Joanne had written when she was younger, she and another girl, and I had rearranged and rewritten so that it was more commercial. At the time it was goin' on, it was probably one of the most terrible experiences in my life. You gotta remember the circumstances surroundin' that. Joanne and I, that was the thing we worked on and developed. You've heard the song. It's "The Red, White, and Blue'll See You Through." It hit number one. It was durin' the Vietnam incident and all the stuff. It was worth about ninety or a hundred thousand dollars. It's about a girl writin' to her boy friend or husband who's a solider in Vietnam. "Oh, the red, white, and blue will see you through. And Uncle Sam'll watch over you. So don't feel frightened, don't be blue." What it is, is an image of a girl fantasizin', talkin' to her lover. She must've thought he was scared he was goin' to die, or maybe she had got a letter from him and he told her about his feelings. And she was tryin' to keep up his feelings, you know, give him some hope and confidence. And she's tryin' to do this with her letter. And her dream, or whatever, is interrupted by the doorbell ringin', and there's a messenger there with a telegram from the armed services and she opens it up and reads it and it says, "We regret to inform you . . ." Then it ends and you play taps. This was the whole thing that we worked out. She and her friend wrote it when they were younger. It had to have impact and punch lines and some musical arrangement, like the taps was my idea. I wanted to do it with a harmonica. And it would've had a lot of impact, especially with Joanne's voice, that thing would've been a skyrocketing hit. We had talked to a lot of people about that song and my plans for it. Joanne sometimes went with me, sometimes she didn't. I was the one to get the doors open.

We talked to a lot of people. Oh, I had a contact in the Wilhelm Agency with the Woburn brothers, and we tried to sell the song there. I got another friend down there called Clyde Beavers. He's got a record company. We pitched it to him, let him listen to it. But I didn't want it to come out on his label because it was too good. He didn't have the distribution and he couldn't support all the big plans that I had. We discussed all these things. I went to Pappy Dailey. I even went to Holland Howard's place. He's a famous country and western songwriter. He went so far as to let us come into Wilderness Publishing Company and use his recording equipment and stuff. And he flipped over the song. He really liked it. And she was with me then. She knew that song was goin'. Ske knew we had a lot of people interested. This is why a lot of people in Nashville, people who are high up in the business, they knew that that was our song and that when it come out we were ripped off.

Well, I drove out one day for some reason to talk to Ginny Johns. I don't know why I ever done it. Thinkin' back on it, I don't know what was my motive. I don't know. But I'd heard stories, like from Clyde Beavers and other people, they'd helped Ginny Johns when she first came to Nashville. They assisted her and helped get her goin' when she had it rough, financially and things. And so I drove out to her farm where she was livin' with her mother and the two girls that she's got. And I told her who I was and what I was doin' and I told her about Joanne and I told her about the song and that a lot of people had heard it. And she says, "It sounds good." And she says, "Describe it to me and tell me what's it about." And I told her how it went "Oh, the red, white, and blue will see you through. And Uncle Sam'll watch over you" and stuff. And I told her about my ideas for the taps and all that. And she says, "Wow, that sounds like it's a real getter. It sounds like it would really have a lot of appeal." And I told her about Joanne and what I wanted to do. And I asked her, you know, if there was any work, if she knew of anybody that needed a steel guitar player or Joanne and I as a team or Joanne as a singer—anything, to be sure and let us know. She said okay.

She just got back from shopping, and she bought a pair of Blue Bell Wrangler jeans, and she tore the back advertisin' label off the jeans and wrote her phone number down on it. I never did call her or see her again except for downtown when she talked to Joanne down at the restaurant in Nashville, when she come off the wall with the stuff about she was thinkin' of quittin' because she missed bein' with the kids. Real slick kid.

Then the song came out. And I couldn't get away from that song. Every place I went in the country, that son of a bitch was playin'. And I'd get physically sick every time I heard that song. My stomach would just . . . And I heard it everywhere, like it was somethin' out to drive me crazy and doin' a good job of it. I wouldn't play that song. And whenever I'd play with a girl singer, I told her not to sing it.

I haven't told many people about that. It's the type of thing where people say, "Hey, listen to this guy. He's tryin' to say he wrote that song." People lie. A lot of guys in the business lie.

The way she recorded it, it's not exactly the way we did it. She changed a few lines and things, but it's the same title, the same story, the same idea, and the same arrangement. And she got it from the discussion I had with her at her house. It's not identical but it's stolen material. What it did was totally ruin what we had. It don't take much if you're a songwriter to do that. All you gotta do is give me a title of somethin' you might be workin' on, and I'll beat you to it. I'd ruin what you're workin' on. Hers was closer than that. It was a direct steal. And there's nothin' you can do about it. In fact, I couldn't even call it a steal. If I did it publicly, she might even be able to say, "Well, where's your proof?" Well, my only proof is that reputable people in the business heard it. I couldn't've sued her. We didn't have copyrighted material. We didn't copyright. I didn't know nothing about that at the time.

The misery of the thing bein' stolen was that Joanne had already gone back to Colorado and I had accepted the fact that her and I wouldn't be gettin' together again. The chances were very, very remote of it. And I was hurtin' from that, hurtin' financially. Then I heard this thing come out on the jukebox and the radio stations and playin' all over the country. And it's ours. It's worth a lot of money. It's something' that if Joanne had done it, everything that we'd worked for would've been obtained. And they even stole my arrangement on the thing, by insertin' the taps at the right place. And I always thought that Joanne had to hear that song. And I always thought she probably figured I had sold it to somebody.

I tried to get ahold of her, but I couldn't find her. I talked with her relatives and things like that. I asked them to relay the message about what had happended to that song, that I damn sure didn't sell it—it was stolen. And to this day I don't know, she might hate me. It's something she conceivably could hate me for.

17

I stayed in Nashville. I moved in with some other musicians. There were five or six of us in the same house, and we all helped each other out. If somebody had money, he'd buy the groceries. He might do it for five or six weeks runnin' 'cause he knew that if his luck changed, he could count on the others to do that for him. It was a real beautiful experience, communal living.

I got on some recording sessions. Some of the records they cut went pretty good across the country, and I was playin' steel on 'em. That made me feel pretty good.

People were talkin' about me, how much I had improved from the time I'd come there and how I was gettin' into the swing of Nashville, which is different from anythin' else. Nashville is far different from your regular grindin' 'em out and gin-mill type thing. This is high-level, professional work. And they party and raise hell a lot, but they're deadly serious. They're always schemin', plannin', and workin' and tryin' to come up with a sound that'll sell a million.

I was doin' good. I wasn't gettin' rich financially but I was gettin' by. And I was gettin' better known all the time. All the steel guitarists down there were startin' to take notice of me—like Buddy Emmons, probably one of the greatest steel guitar players in the world. I played in this club called the Honey Club, and we were playin' authentic country music where a lot of the clubs were hirin' guys and they were showin' off and playin' jazz and stuff and just playin' country when they was on the road. But we kept it country all the time, so we had a hell of a crowd there all the time. And the musicians liked to come there, and the singers, 'cause we were doin' their stuff. I got to meet a lot of 'em there—Jack Greene, Jeannie Seely, Howdie Forrester, a bunch of the fiddle players like Tommy Martin.

There was a girl waitress in there I was datin'. She's the ex-wife of one of the leading musicians, he was a steel guitar player too. Buddy Emmons had told her that if I stayed with it another six months or a year I'd be the hottest thing in Nashville, I'd be the guy they'd all be comin' after for recording sessions and everything. He told the girl that, and she come right over and told me. She says, "Buddy thinks a lot of you. He says you're the one to be watched right now 'cause you're hot."

He told her that all I needed was more equipment, that I was playin' on inferior equipment but that I had a lot of technique and lot of taste and I was puttin' the right things in at the right time and I was fast. And that's what he based his prediction on. Right now it's Louie Green, he's the big name right now in Nashville. His sound is comin' out on most major recordings, but it probably would've been me if I'd stayed there.

She was comin' into a lot of money and she wanted to buy me all new equipment, which I didn't object to at first, because I could've easily paid her back. It would've been just on a loan basis. And I was gonna go along with it, until she slipped and let me know that she wanted me to become super-great on the steel just to put down her ex-husband, just to bust his pride.

I said, "No way. He's a friend of mine. He's a star." And I said, "If that's your motive, then I'm not interested." And I said, "Keep your money."

But she had reasons to be angry too. She'd been brought to Nashville when she was just a kid. She was a Cherokee girl too, like Joanne. Fourteen years old, this guy seduced her and took her to Nashville and got her into prostitution and abandoned her. She became a prostitute. One hell of a girl, though. Do anything for you. And there's a lot of girls down there like that.

I've known a lot of prostitutes, and they like musicians. They'll take care of you when you're down. They're honest people. With people that they like, they're honest. Night people—waitresses, bartenders, prostitutes, musicians—they're kind of in the same clan.

18

I started goin' out on tours with the Grand Ole Opry, and I was all alone. I didn't have any responsibility. I had always been faithful before if I was with a girl—with Joanne and, before that, with my wife, except for that one affair with the neighbor. But no I didn't have nobody, and I was always meetin' women. In that kind of life you're always meetin' women. They're lookin' and you're a musician and that appeals to 'em. And I became a rip-roarin' musician. If I'da been a female, I'd've probably been called a whore. I might not've been chargin' but I'd've had the name put on me.

I remember one night we was playin' a New Year's show at a military base. I was with a Grand Ole Opry group. There was some stars and we played this Air Force base. It was New Year's Eve. The people at the base were TDY to Guam or someplace. Most of the men were gone. For every five people out in the audience, probably three of 'em were women. It was pretty wild, a wild audience, really gettin' with it. They liked the jokes, they liked the music, and they were really participating. And they were hell-raising. That's what they were doing and having a good old time for themselves. It wasn't just goin' out and havin' a few drinks. It turned into like a party. For some reason I wasn't lookin' for any companions that night or to be with anybody. I wasn't even interested, probably because I thought we was going to go back to Nashville as soon as we got done there. So I wasn't lookin' for anything to happen. I was going back with the group. That was my plan, so I didn't try to get anything going.

There were all kinds of offers, parties and things like that. We were all turnin' 'em down. We said we had other commitments and we were sorry but we couldn't stay. That's how it starts out. Usually it's innocent. You know, "Why don't you come up to my house? We got a party goin' and you're welcome." Musicians are welcome to almost any party. And a lot of times a woman will say, "Well, you're goin' out for breakfast afterwards, aren't you? You gotta eat. Rather than go to a restaurant and sit around, it's crowded and people botherin' ya, why don't you come over?" A lot of times it's innocent. You can't always assume it's connected with some kind of sexual thing. A lot of times it's a guy and his wife. They genuinely want you over to their house because they like your music and they are fans and they just want to be friendly.

But when the show ended, we went to the dressing rooms, the large dressing rooms, and the last guy in didn't lock the door. He didn't think about it. He just threw it shut. And we was all in different stages of undress, changin' from our costumes into our street clothes, and the door busts open. Here comes all these women. The dressing room filled up with women, and they were carryin' bottles of booze and all kinds of stuff. It looked like a Roman orgy there for a while, huggin' and kissin' and raisin' hell. And they did talk the leader into stayin' and goin' to a party. We agreed. I met somebody there. I don't even remember who she was or what she looked like or if she was any good.

When you have to be more careful is when you're stayin' in the community, when you're doin' a sit-down job. Now, when you're in a place only one night you're all right, you're in and out of town, you're gone. And nobody expects any more out of ya and there's no involvements and there's no lasting relationships and none expected, though some try to follow ya sometimes. That has happened. But when in the community and you're on what we call a sit-down—that's where you're stayin' a week or more in one place, or months sometimes—you gotta be careful. You gotta be very careful. I had a drummer friend in California, and this guy—I don't know—he was tall and skinny. He had jet black, curly hair and blue eyes. I don't know. He just had a way with women. I don't know what in the hell it was that he had, but they always wanted to take care of him. Rich women wanted to buy him things. This guy could have been a millionaire, and I didn't think he was any better lookin' than anybody else. It was just his ways, I guess. He's sittin' up on the stage one night and in comes his regular girl friend. Then in comes another girl he was with. Before the night was over, before we even got to our second intermission, there was five women in there that he was goin' with and goin' to bed with. And women, bein' women, got to talkin' about guys in the powder room, and one mentioned that she was gonna take the drummer home that night. And his regular girl friend heard her. She says, "Like hell you are." And, needless to say, a brawl started out on the dance floor and all five of them women were in it. And he wouldn't even get off the stage. He asked me what to do. I told him, "I don't know what you're gonna do," but I went out the back door. He was scared. He was really scared. He was a pistol, that guy, Billy Smith. He was from Oklahoma. Good drummer. Hell of a ladies' man.

19

I was doin' good and I got this call one day from my parents, my mother. It'd been years since I'd heard anything from California—my wife. I got this call from my mother that California authorities were tryin' to get in touch with me. She had a name and a telephone number. And I told her that I'd contact 'em and find out what it was about. I thought that perhaps they wanted some money for the support of the children, because, over those lean years, I hadn't been sendin' anything and I hadn't been in touch with her. The last time I had any conversation with her was that time I talked to her in Colorado and she said she was gettin' a divorce.

I called the number and talked to a Darleen Miller at the Los Angeles County Probation Department, Superior Court Probation Department. She went into raptures that I got ahold of her. I told her who I was on the phone. She said, "Oh, thank God you contacted us. We've been worried, and I've been worried sick what to do."

I said, "All right, what's the problem?"

She says, "Well, I don't want you to get all excited until I tell you the whole story." She says, "It's some bad news but it ain't all bad. Things are all right now. It's been bad but it's over." And she says, "I just want to make sure that you can take it."

I said, "Well, what the hell is goin' on?"

She says, "Well, your oldest boy is in McLaren Hall Juvenile Detention Center. And he's just got out of the hospital, he was on the critical list. He's been beaten."

And I says, "What in the hell's goin' on?"

She says, "Well, your wife's boy friend, they were livin' together and he abused the children, beat 'em up pretty bad. The boy was beaten, and the county sheriffs saw him wanderin' around in a dazed condition on the streets and bloodied." He'd gotten away from 'em somehow. The sheriffs picked 'em up. And they had a warrant for 'em and they had to answer charges. I talked to her on a Tuesday and two days later, on a Thursday, they were gonna be arraigned on criminal charges, child-beating to endanger.

I asked how the other children were.

She says, "Well, your second son is fine. He's at home with his mother. And, she says, "of course, you have the little girl at home with you."

I knew somethin' was wrong the minute she said it. I knew the whole story. It just flashed on me, because I didn't have the girl, I never did have the little girl with me. And I questioned her on that. I said, "What are you talkin' about?"

She says, "The little girl you sent for a year ago. You sent some friends out to pick the little girl up. And your wife sent her out to be with you."

I said, "That's not so." And I knew the girl was dead. How I knew I don't know, but I just knew, 'cause why would anybody make up that kinda story unless they were coverin' up somethin' pretty bad? It just came with computer speed in my mind that that's what actually happened.

I told her, I said, "Look," I said, "I don't know if you've got any children or not."

She says, "No, I'm not married." She says, "I don't have any children."

I says, "Does it make any sense to you that a mother with a young child would send it off with friends of a father and let it be gone for a year, and not hear from 'em, and not call it to the attention of some authority?"

She says, "No, it doesn't." She says, "My God." She says, "It sounds terrible."

I says, "I don't have the child. I never sent for the child. I haven't seen the child since I left in 1962."

Now, this was her first case. She was new on the job. She was new in the probation office. In fact, that was her very first case. Instead of waitin' until they had gone into the courts Thursday, and waitin' until the law had 'em in custody, she went that night and confronted 'em with the fact that she had established communication with me and that I had refuted their story about the little girl. She should never have done that because, the minute she left they got in the car and ran. They took my boy with them.

We were makin' a lot of phone calls then. And California was pickin' up the tab on that. I didn't have much money. I explained to her the situation and the business I was in, and I told her I didn't have a whole lot of money. She said that that didn't matter, the state is involved in it now. And in fact the unlawful flight to avoid prosecution was put on 'em and they also put a murder one on 'em, with the evidence that the girl was gone and was last seen in their care in good health, and now the father was a complaining witness and refuting their earlier testimony.

It was a nightmare. I got my oldest boy sent back to New Hampshire to be with my parents. I didn't see him right away. I had commitments and things to take care of, and I didn't think I could do any good in New Hampshire. I was workin' closer with the authorities in the way that I was. And they got a lot of information off me about her relations and where they might be, in Arizona and places like that, possible places where they might go to. And every place I went to, I checked in with the FBI to find out if they had any additional information. There was an all-point, nationwide bulletin on 'em.

20

I met Donna during that time. I met her on a show promotion, I think it was in Indiana. She had graduated from high school the year before, and she was travelin' with a girl friend who knew a promoter from the East Coast, a show promoter from the New York area.

We had a few drinks together, went to movies, one thing and another, partied around, fooled around together. We had sex after a while, not right away. I was still thinkin' a lot of Joanne and she was on my mind. Joanne and I didn't break up in any kind of fight with each other. It's just that she couldn't be away from the kids, and I didn't like it too much but I couldn't knock her for bein' a good mother. I had mixed feelin's on the thing. But the most important thing right then was the situation in California, and I was pretty much frantic over that. I explained it to the girl and she said, "That's terrible." She wanted to know if there was any way she could help. And she fell in love with me pretty fast. She seen me at my best, I guess. She seen me when all the pressure in the world was on me, and she seen me perform, she seen me do things that were very difficult. She was young and impressionable. I wasn't tryin' to impress her, I was just doin' my thing and she happened to be in a good place to observe it.

She thought I was awfully strong. She thought I was pretty courageous. She'd discuss these things with me, and she'd soothe me and console me when I got feelin' bad. Sometimes I'd break down and cry. I wasn't ashamed to cry with her around, because she was just that kind of person. And it wasn't that I was lookin' for sympathy, but I was hurtin' pretty bad, and I probably didn't care if anyone liked it or not. I had to have my cryin' time, gettin' alone somewhere. And she wanted to share that with me too. And she did.

All during that time I had headaches. I had headaches regularly for years. Migraines are terrible. If you never had them, you can't imagine how tough they are. I was ashamed to admit to or give in to the pain 'cause I was always afraid that people would think I was fakin', that nothin' could hurt that much. So I had to cry sometimes. And she observed that, and she consoled me. She said she couldn't imagine what it was like but she knew it had to be terrible. 'Cause she knew I was strong and yet I'd break down like that.

She said, "You're not sure the girl is dead, you know. Maybe she was kidnapped, or maybe she was sold, or maybe the truth will come out." And she gave me other things to think about.

That may have been a possibility, maybe they did need money. I'd heard of people doin' crazy things like that before. And maybe he had talked that nutty thing into sellin' the girl. I hoped that was the case and they'd go tell the truth and we'd go get the child. But in my mind I was pretty sure she had been beaten and had died as a result. I was afraid he might kill the mother and the second child both, 'cause they could testify against him. And, where he was on the run and where he was wanted, he could be desperate enough and dangerous enough to do somethin' like that. I was scared to death all the time that they were gonna find their bodies somewhere. I can't honestly say that I cared if it happened to her, but I damn sure cared if it happened to my son.

21

I got uprooted from Nashville. I was in the show promotion field, and I was amongst musicians well known in Nashville. I was recording as a musician and doing show work as well and toured with some of the Grand Ole Opry shows. But that came to an end because of the California thing. I couldn't keep my work up when all I was thinkin' about was my kids. They were of primary importance. And Donna was of primary importance. Donna was pregnant, and the baby was due any time. So the baby, of course, was important to me. So Donna and I packed and moved to New Hampshire, my home. We waited there to hear somethin' from California. I didn't mind the change. I really didn't. To this day I don't regret it.

One night Darleen Miller called me and she was excited. If I remember right, it just seems like it was night. And she said she had some good news. She was all excited, and she said they had my boy, Benjamin. And then she told me that a couple of off-duty sheriffs were driving on one of the freeways in Los Angeles and by chance were right behind the car, with all of them in it, and they apprehended 'em there. They took my son. Miss Miller had him. I don't know if she took him home with her or what. She said she would be hearing from the attorney general's office on the dates of the trial and that she'd call me as soon as she found out and could arrange to have air fare sent to me so that me and my oldest boy could come to testify.

I was in pretty much of an emotional state. I didn't know what to do. I was pretty sure the girl was dead. And I did have some thought of takin' the law in my own hands in that case, and for a long time I thought to fix it so that there wouldn't be any need for no trial. Like shooting him and her, maybe right in the courtroom. I had the feeling. Donna was aware that I felt that way, and my parents suspected it. They counseled me. I'd get very depressed sometimes over the whole mess, and sometimes I'd let 'em know that I felt I had to do something. Donna for the most part probably had the most influence on me, and she'd tell me that I was important to her and the baby which was comin', and she convinced me how much the boys needed me and that we should let the law take care of it.

It's just as well, 'cause all during the trial they had a couple of great big sheriffs sittin' on either side of me and I couldn't've made a move too much anyway. But she talked me out of it. Donna talked me out of it, and my parents.

I went to California. I was met by Miss Miller, Deputy Sheriff Greeley, and my son Ben. They met us when my son Warren and I got off the plane. They took us that night to a motel to stay, and the boys stayed with me.

So we had quite a reunion, the boys and myself. The boys remembered me 'cause I had been with 'em through their earlier years, until '62. I didn't talk to them about the life they had with their mother and that man. I figured it would be too painful for them to recall it. And they didn't talk about it neither. Even to this day they don't talk about it. It's somethin' that they seem to have masked off. It's their personal way of coping with the situation and adjusting.

I had problems with them during the trial. You see, they were deathly afraid of that person, the guy who had committed those crimes. They were even afraid of him in the courtroom. I did counsel them on that. I said, "Nobody's gonna hurt you anymore." That was the extent of my counseling, but I did counsel them to that extent. I said, "You tell the truth." They were reluctant to go into the courtroom. They didn't want to go. They didn't want to testify, 'cause they were afraid. We're talkin' about eight- and ten-year-old kids now, not much more than infants, and they had suffered pretty much in his hands. I think they had a better idea that their sister was dead because of him than I did. So I told 'em to tell the truth.

In the trial they said they never saw her dead but they saw her beat. And they saw the condition she was in.

It came out in the trial that Cheryl had been beat severely. She was sick for about a week. One day they went to the beach, and the day before he had gone to a hardware store and bought a shovel and put it in the trunk of his car. And they went to the beach, some of his children from his marriage and them and their mother and him. The girl, the baby girl, little Cheryl,—she was four years old—was in the car. They left her in the car. She was sick. She was probably near death then. She didn't go out on the beach, she stayed in the car. The kids remember bein' at the beach most of the day and gettin' in the car and ridin' up to the mountains. And they fell asleep. They remember bein' awake on the return trip and Cheryl wasn't with 'em. But they didn't see anyone bury her or kill her or do anythin'. But they knew that they had that trip to the beach and she was with 'em, then they went to the mountains, and when they come back she wasn't with 'em. And this was just about the extent of their testimony in the courtroom, which isn't really enough for a conviction on first-degree murder, not in California at least. They needed much more than that.

I got to meet the deputy district attorney who would be prosecuting the case. Now, nobody, nobody has any sympathy for anyone that murders four-year-old children or beats children. You can form a comradeship with an armed robber. He can be a comic. He can be all kinds of people. He can be like your best friend maybe. And you can have tolerance for him commitin' that kind of a crime. But the crime of hurtin' women and children is usually not tolerated, even by the toughest convicts. When guys go into prison with that kind of rap on 'em, they don't have it very easy. Nobody likes 'em. And the prosecutor didn't either. California was goin' for murder one and askin' for the death penalty. That's what they wanted on both of 'em. They couldn't produce the body. They couldn't find out the exact location from the children. They were asleep when they got up to the mountains.

She was very smart. She was very, very smart, 'cause she knew they were safe if she didn't testify against him. She proclaimed an undying love for him and all types of things. I got letters she wrote to me afterward, about how much she loved him and needed to help him, that would turn your stomach. She wouldn't tell the truth. She wouldn't tell the authorities what had happened.

So they went to trial with me as a complaining witness. About all I could contribute to the trial was that I had never sent for the girl by any friends. I remember that I said on the stand that I wished I had, that unfortunately I didn't. And their lawyers screamed because I added that tag on it, and the judge overruled the objections. He said, "That's his feeling, and he's got a right to express it." 'Cause I wish I had sent for the little girl. We wouldn't all be there that day and gone through those things. She'd still be alive.

Well, they got all the testimony they wanted from the boys and myself. I was anxious to get out of there. I wasn't really sure I could control myself forever on the thing, and it was a bad situation to be in. I wanted to get back to New Hampshire with the boys and start buildin' my home with Donna and the baby and be around my family. I told 'em I was anxious to get out of there. And they felt that even though the trial wasn't complete, they had no more need for our testimony. Any further testimony wouldn't be of any help. So between the probation department and the district attorney they agreed that we could, probably should, return to New Hampshire as a family, with the stipulation that we'd speedily return in case somethin' developed in the case where we was needed and further testimony was needed. I told 'em we certainly would, that we were just as anxious for justice in the thing as they were. So we returned to New Hampshire.

Well, they questioned her, and they tried to talk her into telling 'em exactly what happened and where the little girl was, if she wasn't harmed. There was always the chance that she had let some relative, some distant relative in some faraway state or somethin', take care of the kid. They were worried about that, the state was. They said, "It is a possibility, you know. We could come outa this lookin' real bad."

I said, "I don't care what you look like. I hope they do produce it."

They said, "Well, we do too, of course, but we have to be careful from a legal standpoint how far we go and how hard we bear down. We have accused 'em of murder." They felt that that was enough to make 'em do somethin'. And a normal person, if the girl was alive, it would've.

22

We left the state and came back to New Hampshire, but within a week I got a call from Darleen Miller. She called and said the trial was over. She says,"You're probably not gonna be satisfied, but she was sentenced to a year and he was sentenced to five to fifteen years, for involuntary manslaughter." I asked her what happened. I was very upset. I was angry. I couldn't believe it, that somebody could do somethin' like that to children and get off like that.

She says, "Well, you have to understand that the trial couldn't last any longer. It had to come to an end, one way or another. And the prosecution had a very weak case for murder because she wasn't testifying, she wouldn't divulge any information, they didn't have no body and no knowledge of any whereabouts of the body. The only thing they had was that they had established that the child was last seen with them, when she was alive. And that's all. That's not really strong enough for first-degree murder. So the state had to agree to the lesser charges before they would be willing to cooperate, tell 'em where the girl was and once they agreed to the lesser charges and they got sentenced, the double jeopardy clause came into play and they couldn't be tried again for the same crime. And they agreed to show 'em where the little girl was." I think it was the next day, and she said she'd be in touch with me.

They did go up, and Darleen described that they looked around, they didn't know exactly where it was, but they did take them to her gravesite. And I made her tell me about it. I wanted to know. The girl had been murdered and buried up in the mountains.

I immediately thought about bringin' her back, perhaps havin' her cremated out there and have her ashes brought back and have her buried near my grandmother and grandfather in the cemetery. I felt like we could go there sometimes, the boys and I. They could visit the grave. I thought it would be helpful to them, and I just wanted it. I don't know why, but I did.

I asked Darleen about the grave, and she said the baby had been put in a shallow grave up in the mountains and they got the baby's blanket and evidence that she had been buried, and she was pretty vague on things. I asked her about the return of the body. And she said she didn't know anything about that and she didn't have any experience in it and I'd probably have to work out something with somebody in the business here, the funeral business, and some people out in California.

That bothered me. Mr. Williams, Ralph Williams, in Dover, has a funeral home. He's been known in the family for years, and I called him and asked him about it. I think he's the one that told me, or maybe it was Darleen, I'm not sure. Anyway, one of 'em told me that she had been buried in a shallow grave and then animals had tore the grave up. There wasn't much left. There was only a few parts there, and he didn't think it would really be worth the expense and everythin' to me to have it brought back. He was very kind and he was very understanding and he offered to me what he thought was the best counsel at the time. He said, "It might even be the best thing if you don't do what you plan to do. It might have a harmful effect on the boys instead of the beneficial effect that you feel it might have." He says, "Nobody can predict those things." He says, "It might have been helpful, but it could have been harmful too." So he says, "Why don't you just leave things alone and forget about that?"

I had to, really. I didn't have any choice.

23

When Darleen and I talked about the sentencing, her and I both agreed that that wasn't much time for either one of the parties. His name's Howard Moore Thomas. I haven't mentioned his name. I don't know why. I don't like his name much probably. He's the one that got the five to fifteen, and she got a year. I expressed my amazement at that sentence. I said, "That doesn't seem very wise." And I computed in my head the fact that they would be both on the street when the children were still of tender years.

She said, "Well, that's right."

I said, "He don't seem normal to me, what I saw of him in the courtroom." And I knew that this wasn't the first time he had been known to harm children. When he was seventeen, he had taken an infant baby out of a bassinette on somebody's porch and beat it unmercifully. So I said, "I can't help but wonder how predators like that can exist on the face of the earth, human predators, somebody who can hurt a four-year-old girl, somebody who can take an infant baby out of a bassinette and beat on it. I don't know if I could apprehend a person like that, if I was a police officer, without blowin' his head off on the spot. I wouldn't trust myself." I said, "And that monster's gonna be out on the streets in a few years."

She says, "Well, maybe not, but there is a possibility that he will be." And she says, "Why, anyway?"

I said, "Well, I feel there's a chance, with this type of person, who's already done what he'd done, he might want to take some retaliation against the boys for testifyin' or for knowin' what they already know about him or somethin'." I said, "I

69

have no fear of him personally, but I work, I'm away from home, and I don't want my family threatened by this creep. If I was there I'd shoot him on the spot, but I'm not always home. I'd love to have a confrontation with him but not involving the family."

She says, "I can see your point." She says, "Just to be on the safe side and to have more power if such a thing should happen or if the children are kidnapped or harmed in any way, how about if I have the court maintain jurisdiction over them so that if anyone does try to hurt them the powers of the courts of California can come into play on it too."

I said, "That sounds all right to me." Which it wasn't all right. It wasn't legal and it wasn't smart. But with the mood of that moment and with the things we was discussing, I didn't at all anticipate any problems coming from that.

I should never've had this discussion with her. It was just a spur-of-the-moment thing, and it had far-reaching effects on our lives after that. She didn't intend for that to happen. I know she didn't. She'd tell you the same thing today if you could talk to her. She didn't intend to happen what did happen. I know it because she really liked the boys. She got very attached to the boys and the family and the case. She got very much personally involved. She even cried and the kind of things you might do if you were involved in something like that closely. When we were out there for the trial, she'd take the boys to lunch or go with us to lunch and make sure that they didn't want for anything or need for anything. She was always concerned about 'em. She loved 'em very much. But the phone calls dwindled off, and she was out of the picture for a very long time.

Well, I was left with a problem, a very, very serious problem. The boys were maintained under the jurisdiction of the California court. The state of New Hampshire's probation department was requested by their court's probation department to keep a check on the boys. Pretty soon it became like the boys were criminals. It became like they were somethin' the courts were really watching close for some wrong that they had done. And this is the way it developed, it really did. It wasn't like they were victims of some horrendous thing that had happened to 'em and they were bein' protected by the courts—in no way at all. They had to be checked in their school records. The probation department of New Hampshire was allowed to come into my home. I cooperated with them at first, and they took full advantage of it. They had no business in my home. The boys were New Hampshire residents, and the California courts had no legal say over them.

It got pretty bad. They started goin' down to their schoolrooms, and I told 'em I didn't want them near their schools. I said, "The boys have done no wrong." I got angry. I says, "You're treatin' 'em like criminals." I said, "They are the victims." And I didn't want 'em in the schools, but they did go into the schools one time, one of the New Hampshire probation officers. I got on him about it, and he agreed that it was probably wrong and he'd check with me in the future and make sure that all his visits were at home, 'cause I knew that kids could be vicious, and if it was known that a probation officer was down there lookin' in on 'em then they'd be tormented by their classmates, 'cause their classmates wouldn't understand.

The boys were havin' enough trouble at school as it was without having the probation officers make things worse. They were having trouble adjusting at school. Because of the kinds of things they had seen and been involved in, they were in a depressed way for a long time. It was hard for 'em in school. I had trouble with some of their teachers because of that. I went to the school and explained what had happened. I told 'em I didn't care if the boys failed that year of school, that their personal adjustment and family adjustment was much more important than that year in school. They could make that up after they got adjusted. Most of the people cooperated except for one teacher who got weepy over the thing and tried to pamper Warren and mother him. He took to that like a duck to water, and it did mess him up in school. He needed discipline there and love at home. She tried to play the parent role, and she made a mistake and admitted it afterward. I got very angry about that and went down and confronted her with it, and she realized she made a mistake. 'Cause when Warren didn't want to do his work so much and he felt like he could go to her for shelter and warmth and protection and love and all that stuff. I told her that wasn't her job. He job was to be a teacher. But the damage was done. I had a hell of a job on my hands, as you can see and imagine.

I got a phone call one afternoon from the probation department in California, inquiring about the boys. I told 'em they've been gettin' their reports, or I suppose they were gettin' their reports since the New Hampshire probation department was keepin' a check on things, which I resented but I still felt it was necessary by law. Since then I have found out it was not necessary by law. The New Hampshire probation department was way out of line. All these things was workin' on me, and there's anger in me now over it. It was eatin' on me inside. It was a threat to my family's security and my children. It wasn't a personal threat to me, but it was disrupting what I wanted to be a way of life in my family, and I didn't think anyone had a right to do that. I felt the law was wrong in that, and I've come to find out there's no such law.

This phone call I got was from my ex-wife's social worker. She was released, or was gettin' ready to be released, and he wanted the boys to go out there for a visit to be with their mother, for her rehabilitation.

I said, "You surely must be joking." I hit the roof. I said, "I don't personally care about her rehabilitation. I'm too busy with the boys' adjustment, and they're comin' along fine and they don't need her. If she needs them, that's tough, 'cause she had them once and she abused them. Their sister's dead thanks to her and the way she lived."

He said, "Well, she is not going to hurt the children. She is not a brutal person. There's no reason to think that."

I says, "If you let a brute in, you're brutal."

He said, "She might've been afraid of him too, you know."

I said, "They were in her care and responsibility, and there's plenty of law in California that she could've went to for help if she really wanted it. You can't tell me she was afraid of him, 'cause he wasn't with her twenty-four hours a day. He didn't keep her chained in a closet. When he left, she could have went to the proper authorities and had all kinds of protection. I don't buy the fear theory." I said, "I just can't picture someone not protectin' their children. In my mind a mother in that kind of a situation dies first before she allows it to go one second further."

He said, "You're being too hard on her."

I said, "In the weeks before she died, there was testimony that the girl was covered with bruises, black and blue, even down inside her ear was all black and blue. There was hemorrhaging inside there. And my ex-wife's own sister testified to that, and she questioned her on it. And she'd say that the girl had been bumped by a car and knocked down rather hard, but that she felt she was all right. Didn't even take her to the doctor. Didn't even do that much. Didn't try to save the baby." I said, "You're makin' a mistake in thinkin' she's a human being. She's some kind of creature, a creature that shouldn't be let alone with children." I said, "You don't know what you're foolin' with." I said, "Those children are more important than her to me, and they should be to you."

He says, "Well, she is important. She is my client."

I like to broke his jaw. I told him if he wanted trouble he'd get it. I says, "I'm not willing to let those boys get on no plane to go see her." I says, "When they get older, when they can decide for themselves . . ." I says, "You can tell her this. You can know it for your records. When they are strong enough to handle that emotional experience, and if they wish to see her again—and I'm not even sure they do—then they can go to her and I won't do a thing against it." I said, "I've not said anything against her to them. I've not even mentioned her name to them. It's like she doesn't even exist. Whatever they know about her and whatever feelings they have for her, she had to put them there when she had 'em and when she was supposed to be a mother to 'em. I've done nothin' for her or against her since they've been with me. I don't even mention her name, because I don't want the memories of California comin' up."

And that is the truth, I didn't. I didn't let her communicate with them, because of their adjustment thing not because of any hatred for her, because I didn't think it was wise to let her be antagonizin' the boys with letters and stirrin' up memories that I didn't even have a notion of. She did write a couple of letters, and I did keep 'em from 'em for that sole purpose, that they were

73

in a terrible emotional state at that time and I didn't feel like they could adjust with that kind of an influence on 'em.

I told him these things. I said, "When they get older, if they want to see her, if they want to go to California, I'll work my fingers to the bone if I have to and pay their way out there. But when they are little children like they are now and they need my protection, they're gonna get it." And I says, "Somethin' in me tells me not to let them go to California." And I says, "I'm not gonna let them go."

He couldn't see none of that. He threatened. I'm talking about a period of time now. I kept up a front of bravado but inside I was gettin' pretty soft. I was gettin' scared. I was gettin' weak. Every time the phone rang, my blood would be like ice water. I was frightened. Until you have children and they're seriously threatened by something like that, you don't know what fear is. I've been afraid, in my life, of personal danger of somethin' goin' wrong or gettin' hurt or almost drownin'. I know those kind of fears. But it don't compare with the kind of fear that you have when a couple of your children are in a very serious danger. There's no fear like that. I probably should have had a nervous breakdown, but I didn't. I don't know why I didn't. In a way I think I went crazy through it all. In that area, I think I was crazy. I sure was distraught and didn't know where to go, where to turn to. I knew I couldn't trust the New Hampshire authorities because I was judging all of them by the actions of the probation department. I felt like they were right in it with California, and California in fact told me they were. This guy's name was David Becker, her social worker. He said, "Well, if you don't cooperate, then I'll just have to go to the courts and get a warrant, and New Hampshire authorities will take the children by force if necessary and put 'em on a plane, and they will come out here."

I said, "I'll die the day that happens."

24

So that was botherin' me. I didn't really know what to do. I needed help but I didn't know what was available to me. I had fallen away from the Mormon Church. I done a lot of talkin' with the Lord, but I didn't know there were friends in the Church who were just as concerned about me as they were their own lives. I didn't know about the law. I didn't know any of these things. And I was desperate all this time. All through the time I was involved in the criminal activity, I had this fear and this anger.

It wasn't until I got into prison that I began concentrating on the legal side of the problem. I had the time, and it was always on my mind. I'd fall asleep readin' law books to find out how I could protect them boys against the state of California. That's how I became a jailhouse lawyer. I had studied a little bit of law in California, but that was Business Law I and II, not criminal law and not constitutional law. To protect them against Becker forcin' their removal from the state of New Hampshire, I researched the law the best I could. I talked with people that impressed me that they might know a little bit about the law. I talked with them in depth about all kinds of things about the law so I could get a better understanding of how it worked and how you got things filed under courts.

I studied and I read and I checked on the law, and I liked some of the things that I found in the law. I filed a motion in the federal court in Concord, and they replied that they didn't have any jurisdiction over California. So I asked them, "Who in the hell does if you don't?" So that raised a legal question: Where do I go for relief? And I think it was a court of proper jurisdiction, where I am a New Hampshire resident and the children are. They didn't want to get into the issue of that. I was going to appeal it to the first circuit court in Boston. I didn't have to, though, because the magistrate sent a lawyer friend over to talk to me. He asked me the problem 'cause they could see by the writings that I was very concerned and that there probably was a serious problem. And I really laid it to him. He said there was a hearing coming up. Every so often they'd have a review in the courts. And there was a notice of the hearing that came, certified, to me. They advised me to petition the courts out there, which I did. I sent it to the judge out there, by mail. I told him that I couldn't appear in person but that I was representing myself. I related to him what had actually happened in the boys' lives and the murder of their sister, the parties involved, and that I worried that she would try to appear in his courtroom at that hearing to try to get permanent custody. I suspected that they were going to try that. I wrote the whole record out for the judge. I gave the judge four or five pages of testimony on the conditions—the trial, the adjustment of the boys after they got back here, how well they responded to the love that they got from their new mother Donna, how much they loved their baby sister, who I felt might have helped in some way replace the one they lost. And I wrote down where I felt that the courts never did in fact have jurisdiction once the boys were sent to reside with me in New Hampshire, that California lost all rights and interest in them when they legally left the state. And the court sent back a decision that they had dismissed all further interest and jurisdiction over the boys, and I felt that was a win. And it was, 'cause the threat was over. That was in 1971 or almost 1972. I went through hell every night in this prison until that decision was reached, expectin' to be told any moment that the boys had been grabbed up. If somethin' like that had happened, I would have escaped. I would've went to California and shot her. I definitely would've or I would've been shot down in the process. I would've definitely tried that. I would die for my children. I sure would.

Part II

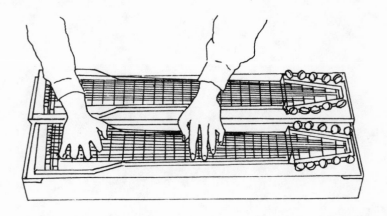

1

It was rough for me in New Hampshire. I wasn't workin' steady. I'd do odd jobs here and there, pickin' up what I could for income. Like I'd help a friend, he raised chickens. He'd pay me a little bit. I'd do it as much to help out as I did to get the pay, 'cause he couldn't pay me a full salary and he couldn't afford a hired hand. He needed some help and I needed some help, so we both profited by it.

I started playin' music where I could and when I could 'cause I always could depend on that, it seemed. I was pretty good. I got a band together. I was the leader of it. And by 1970 the band got established in the area. The band was popular, and I was popular as a band leader and a musician. Jimmy Wilson was in it, my childhood friend. He played guitar and sang. And we got some others together who wanted to play full-time, and I knew we could do better full-time in music than by bein' janitors in some factory. We built a group that thought that way and we did well, we got the bookings.

We began doin' sit downs. We were stayin' in one place all the time. We'd leave our equipment set up in one lounge in Portsmouth week after week after week, and the owners liked us to be there like that 'cause the place was packed every time we were there, the place was like New Year's Eve. And I'm not braggin', people will tell you that knew the band in those days.

In the lounge where we did most of our playin', the owners didn't have just the lounge license. They had a restaurant license. And to justify the lounge, they had to have the restaurant or the liquor commission would yank their license. The owner was upset 'cause the liquor commission had started to prod him a little bit, 'cause the activity of the restaurant wasn't up to what they considered standard requirements or what the hell ever. Plus the fact that people that had an in with the commission, competitors of this lounge where we was workin', were complainin' because this place was gettin' too much business due to the popularity of the band. I know that. It's politics and it's vicious and it's corrupt, and it shouldn't be allowed. I know that his competitors tried to get at him and have his license removed to put him out of business 'cause he was drawin' all the crowd, and the only way they could do it was through the liquor commission. The owner couldn't handle it. He was worried. And there was a little discussion after hours and during the day and things like that where he'd say, "I'm worried I'm gonna have to close unless I can do somethin' with the restaurant." It wasn't open enough hours and there wasn't enough variation on the menu and things like that. He was gettin' frantic.

So I asked him why didn't he just operate the restaurant. He said he couldn't. So it come down to the fact that I'd take over. It would be mine. Everything was in his name, but the restaurant was mine. I didn't get any help from him financially.

And the restaurant didn't make any money. It lost money. It always did. I had to make it up out of my pay, so that I wasn't able to pay my bills around the house. And that, plus my problems protecting my children from the authorities in California and New Hampshire, made me scared and nervous. But I couldn't let Donna see this. I couldn't let the family know that things weren't stable, that things were in jeopardy. I didn't figure it was manly of me or the right thing to put that kind of burden on other people. It was my problem.

I didn't always have the money to pay the employees of the restaurant, the waitresses and cook and dishwashers. And sometimes I'd have to ask 'em to wait. Some went along with me, but others said, "No, I want my pay." And I'd have to get it out 'cause there are pretty strict laws on people's pay.

I had to buy the raw materials, the supplies. I didn't know anything about it, but I had to go out and beat the bush and find venders that sold wholesale. I had to go down to the meat distributors. I had to go to vegetable people. I was busy all the time. I always had something on my mind to do, connected with the restaurant. I played with the band at night, so I didn't get much sleep. I was takin' naps mostly. And the restaurant wasn't doin' well at all. It was constantly, constantly losin' money. I'd get nervous and desperate. I'd think, if only there was some way I could get some money.

I had a lot of ideas about makin' the restaurant successful. My head was filled with ideas, in fact. If I had some operatin' capital, I'm sure that would've been the finest little eatin' establishment in the state today. For instance, I had the idea to move a rotisserie type thing up in front of the window and feature roast beef and steaks and things and have the cooking done right in front of the window and an exhaust fan puttin' a little bit of the smell out on the street so people could smell the aroma of the cooking foods. That was one little gimmick that I wanted to do, but that would cost a couple thousand dollars to set up that display thing where the cooking was done right in the window. That would've went over big, I'm sure.

I wanted to do some advertising but I never had the money to put into it. Little gimmicks. I thought too of later on gettin' Nashville stars in once a month and the overflow from the lounge would support the restaurant. And I'd put their pictures up in the restaurant and have them around talkin' to the customers. The place would've been packed twenty-four hours a day if we'd've developed that kind of business. But I didn't have the capital.

I knew I had to come up with something to improve the restaurant—not improve it as far as food was concerned, though. There was tremendous food. I don't know why people didn't catch onto that. I did get a cook to come down and help me, and the guy was really a blessing 'cause he loved to cook and he liked the band and he liked me and Jimmy. He came lookin' for some extra work and he saw the conditions and he said, "Look, you can't pay me a cook's wages but just give me a little bit to cover my expenses." He just wanted a little money. He didn't charge me what a chef would charge. And this guy could make homemade rolls and breads and things like this.

We took some friends of the band that used to come to our dances and liked us a lot. They all owned horses and belonged to a riding club. They wanted to have their awards and a banquet and everything at our place, and I never set up a banquet before. Well, he took over, this young guy, and he set the banquet up and it went off without a hitch. It was beautiful.

The food was superb there because I bought all the best things. Like when I grilled my hamburgs, for example, there would always be a little dusting of garlic powder to just accent your taste buds. Little things. And I would brown the rolls in pure butter. And when I made home fries, I didn't use grease from the kitchen or oil, it was pure butter. Everything was delicious in there. The toast was hot and had real butter on it. The best-quality foods were bought, the very best vegetables, the very best meats. But it just didn't go.

2

Early on, when I got involved in the restaurant, somebody I knew in the town, that knew the band and that knew me—I can't remember just who it was—said, "I know a guy, Tom Walker, and he needs a job. He just got paroled and he needs a job. He has to be workin' and a place to stay or he'll have to go back to prison."

I told the guy, I says, "Look, I ain't makin' no money. The restaurant's not payin' off."

He says, "Yeh, but it's a job." He thought we could work somethin' out, 'cause Tom would have to go back to prison if he didn't have employment and a place to stay. He says, "I can't speak for him but I think you guys could work somethin' out. Why don't you talk to him?"

I says, "Well, have him come over." And right away I liked the guy. He was a personable guy. He was well groomed, neat and clean, and seemed to have a good head on him. He was smart. And he was a pretty good-sized guy, you know, he could handle any trouble in the restaurant when I wasn't there. I was sure of that. And he was straightforward. He seemed to be pretty honest with me. I took a liking to him right away and we did get along good from the start. He was glad we could work out something to the satisfaction of his parole board.

I told Tom, "If you need an address, I could set you up with that. I can give you enough money to get an apartment." I told him what the scoop was on the restaurant. I said, "It's not making a damn penny." I told him, "If you want to go in there and if you want to help me, I'll split right down the line with you." I said, "The only reason I'm concerned about the restaurant being open is because the band is working in the lounge and if the lounge closes down, the band is out on the street. The whole business would shut down."

He thought it was a pretty good deal. He was willing to invest his time. And he did a real honest effort. After we had that going, the parole department knew he was working there, and everything was okay.

Tom had no problems. He had no troubles. Then one day some people came to the restaurant and told him he was wanted. In a certain town the police wanted him. He asked me, "What should I do?"

I said, "Well, you should contact them. But first, where you are on parole, I would call them and find out what it is about."

Well, he did. He called them. And they said, "Never mind what it is about. We think you know what it is about. Just come on down and see us. We want to see you down here."

And I got on the phone with the chief and I asked him if it was anything serious. And he said, "Yeah, it could be pretty serious."

I said, "Well, when do you want him down there?"

He said, "Right away."

I said, "Well, he wants to have the benefit of counsel with him where he's on parole. And I've advised him to do that and to make contact with a bondsman." So that in the event that any action was taken immediately, he'd be taken care of.

He said he had no objections to that. He said, "How long would it take to do it?"

I said, "Within a day, no more than two."

He said, "All right." He didn't even bother to ask where Tom was because he knew Tom couldn't get very far.

Tom was charged with participation in a burglary in the nighttime, and on the day and time it was supposed to have occurred he was working in the restaurant. I had sales slips where he had gone to the market and purchased goods for the restaurant. He didn't have an automobile at the time, and I didn't have one at the time. We were using a taxi to pick up our goods. We had all these people that could testify. We had the store clerk. We had the taxi driver. We had the patrons at the restaurant and bar and we had the bartender and waitresses. We had probably a couple hundred people that could testify where he was on that particular date and time, and they still convicted him of this so-called robbery. I testified at his trial as an alibi witness and I told the truth, but they implicated that it was me probably driving the car for him and the other guy. And I was on stage at the time playing music. I was pretty hostile.

Another thing. After the police officially charged him with the crime, a police officer testified that he saw him at the scene, which he didn't. He couldn't have seen Tom there because Tom wasn't there. It might have been somebody that looked like him, but I seriously doubt it. It was a setup all the way. It was obviously a setup.

He asked me what he should do. When it came down to the end, the state offered a deal of one to three years, I think, if he would plead guilty, cop a plea.

I said, "Tom, you're not guilty. How in the hell can you plead guilty to something you didn't do?"

He said, "Man, you don't know what it's like. I'm on parole and I've been to prison for these kind of crimes." He said, "I think I'd better plead guilty."

I said, "Well, I can't tell you not to. I can't tell you what to do, but I'll be damned if I'd plead guilty to something I didn't do." I pointed out that there was plenty of people that knew where he was at the time.

He said, "Well, you're right." So he pleaded not guilty and he wound up being found guilty by the jury and got three to five.

84

Well, I felt very bad for him and his family. I took his wife in with my family for a while. But not too long after he got sent up to prison on the robbery charge, his wife broke up with him.

3

I met people through the jail system in the process of visiting Tom. People reach out from behind the screens. "Will you do this for me?" "Will you do that for me?" "Would you make a phone call, let my people know I'm all right?" "Would you call my wife and make sure she comes up on a certain day?" Or it could be a call to the lawyer, getting little goodies for them—hot chili peppers, any friggin' thing—and letting their wives bring it to them. A guy in prison appreciates any little thing. It don't take much. The least little thing a guy would remember forever, if he's doin' time.

There were these two guys especially, Vince and Joey, and they'd say, "Hey, we're getting out of here. We're gonna beat this rap. Anything we can do for you later, we'd be glad to do it." And they were people who were in a position where they could back up what they could say. I didn't know their background. I didn't try to find out, but I knew they were criminals. And Tom told me they were. He said, "They're heavy people."

And they'd say, "Is there anything we can do to help you?"

And I'd say, "Well, I don't think so." But every time I'd see them, I'd think about goin' into crime with them. They weren't askin' me to commit crimes with 'em, but I was thinkin' about it. And I was really susceptible to that idea. The restaurant was failing and Tom was gone, a terrific injustice. Maybe I had to do what I finally did to save my mind, I don't know. I couldn't stand no more of the way it was. I had to do something. I should have went to church. But I got away from the Church. I got away from it. I started to think for myself and I thought I could handle everything for myself alone. A man's on his way down when he starts thinking that way. He fights hard but it's a losing

85

battle. When a guy thinks he's alone, that's when he's in trouble. That's when he needs counseling the most, but he won't take it and he probably doesn't know where to go for it.

I wanted to join their side. I wanted to get off Nixon's side and get on their side. I don't see too much damned difference between the two, except one you go to prison for and the other you don't.

Tom had told them some of the things I did for him, both during the time he was a parolee and also during his court experience, and they liked it. They thought I was a solid dude. And I am, in prison vernacular, a standup guy, solid people, somebody you can depend on, somebody who'd keep his mouth shut, somebody who'd help you if he can and damned sure won't hurt you. And they felt me out. They knew that I was bitter. They knew the story of what happened in California, because they rapped with Tom in the jail. I know they knew 'cause they discussed it a little bit. They said, "That was pretty bad. Yeah, we heard about that, yeah." I told them a little bit. They said, "Yeah, we know. Tom told us." They knew everything about me. And they sincerely wanted to do me a favor. And they were sincere. They come to me and they says, "Look, if there's anything we can do for you, if anyone's giving you any trouble—anything. If you need some money . . ." They knew the business was in trouble.

I said, "No." I was stubborn. I was proud. But I got to thinking, maybe they're experienced. I'm not experienced. I could learn from them. I'd have their protection, their contacts. I had studied the statistics of the FBI, how so many people get caught on this kind of crime and so many people get away with it. It's printed in *Time* magazine. It's printed in the *Boston Globe*. So I thought abut what was the best thing to get into, and I felt sure I'd get away with it. I decided I was going to be a criminal. I had the opportunity through them.

Finally I said, "I want some action."

They said, "What are you talkin' about?"

I said, "I want to make some money."

They said, "What kind of money' What are you talkin' about?"

I said, "Big money." I said, "I'm talkin' about robberies. That's what I'm talkin' about."

They said, "You ever done anything like that before?

I said, "No."

They said, "You don't even know what you're talkin' about."

And I said, "No, but I think you do.

They said, "Yeah, we do."

And the funny thing is, I didn't have to do anything wrong with them. They didn't expect that of me. They were really concerned about me. Many times, before we done one thing, they said, "Are you sure?" And before we did do anything, they said, "Are you sure you want to do this?"

Tom warned me not to get involved with them. He said, "Stay away from them."

I told Tom some of the things I had been thinking. I said, "Look, the whole United States of America, its government, its business, and everything else is set up on criminal activity. I said, "This country's run like a damned crap game. The house has got all the money and there's no way you're gonna win. What makes Kennedy, Johnson, those people in the government and industry think that they can have that big chunk of the money? What makes them think they can have it all and give nothing in return?" I knew that Nixon was no good. I knew that politics in Washington was corrupt. But people read about these things and they forget them. They forget the things that Jack Anderson is telling them and Drew Pearson before him. And I said to Tom, "Don't you realize what these people are doing? Don't you know that Lyndon Johnson used the Federal Communications Commission and set his wife up with all kinds of businesses?" I said, "So far as that goes, so far as deserving goes, I feel that every bank in the United States deserves to be robbed once every hour."

Tom said, "Don't get involved too much. Don't get involved too deep. Don't use a gun."

I thought, fuck it. What's he know?

4

They beat their rap soon after that. And one day I got to the restaurant and the bartender comes over to me and says, "You got some important visitors." I asked him what he was talkin' about and he tells me how two guys came in and asked where I was. They left a message they'd call me. They didn't leave their names. The bartender said they had a Cadillac, a black one, and they didn't even bother to find a parkin' space for it, they just double-parked in front of the restaurant, left it out in the street and come in after me.

A little later I got a call. It was Vince, and he said he was sorry they missed me. He said, "You got a swell spread there." He was talkin' about the restaurant. Then he asked me if I was serious about bein' partners with them or if I had changed my mind. I said, "Damned right I'm serious." He says, "Okay, let's talk some more about it."

I remember the first time we met was at a restaurant downtown, in Portsmouth. Only we didn't go in there. I waited for them out front. There was a menu posted on the window and I looked at it, as if I was deciding what to order. When they drove up, it was like old friends meeting and we shook hands and they asked how I was and said, "It's good to see you, kid."

Then we went for a ride. Actually, they had me drive. One of 'em, I think it was Vince, said, "Let's see you handle the wheels." They'd give me directions down to Massachusetts where they lived, first to Joey's house and then to Vince's. They lived in the suburbs outside of Boston.

I drove a couple of times. I figured they wanted to see what kind of driver I'd make for when we'd do a job. And we'd go to Massachusetts each time, drivin' around, have coffee somewhere, have lunch or somethin'.

They're talkin' to me all the time now. They've become my teachers. They tell me they do this, they do that. They trusted me an awful lot, 'cause I could have been a cop.

One of the things they explained to me right at the start was not to talk to them about any of our business on their home phones. They told me they thought the police had their phones tapped. I was to call 'em, talk about the weather or sports or something, and then hang up. They'd call me right back from another phone.

They'd tell me about how, when you do a job, you always use a stolen car, which they called a hot box, and to wear gloves, and to have your own car parked somewhere pretty far from the scene of the crime so you could drive the hot box to it, jump out, and be gone without anybody bein' able to connect you with the car. They asked me if I had a record. I said, "No. In fact, I've never even been fingerprinted."

They said, "Are you sure? You've never been in the service or anything like that?"

I said, "No."

They said, "Well, that's beautiful." And it was. I was worth a lot to 'em. They said we'd probably start out locally, around where they lived in Massachusetts, to see how we worked to-gether and how serious I was about it. Then we'd go do some things, really big jobs, outside the state. They said they were too hot in Massachusetts, the police knew 'em and how they oper-ated, and they'd be picked up right off. They said I might have to do most of the work at first, but it wouldn't be too long before we'd be doin' things outside of the area. For instance, they told me they had information about a shipment of diamonds comin' in by courier to the airport in New York, and it was easy, and we were gonna do it. There would be a lot of money in it for all of us.

They told me how important it was, if I got caught, not to say anything about who was in it with me, and I said, "You don't even have to tell me that."

They said, "We can see that we don't." They said that who-ever gets caught can count on the others to get the bail money together and get a lawyer and pay the lawyer's fees, if it was at all possible to do that. And they said, "We'll split everything we make three ways." All of that sounded good to me. And it sounded to me like they knew what they was doin' and I had a good chance with them.

I was already startin' to count all the thousands and thou-sands of dollars and dreamin' about what I'd spend it on. I'd have several houses—a ranch out west and another house in New Hampshire. I was gonna take my family on trips to Europe and Bermuda and places like that every year. I was thinkin' of buyin' out the restaurant and the bar and fix it up, bring in the big name bands and stars from Nashville, and I'd set up my own band, and maybe I'd get into prostitution and gamblin' where there weren't so many risks and I'd have enough money really to protect myself. I could pay to have a hospital build a children's wing and I figured no judge is gonna sentence a man to prison who's got the children's wing of a hospital named after him. My boys were gonna be senators. All these things was goin' through my head, and I couldn't wait to get started.

We'd talk about sports, about fishin', one thing and another. It was during the time I knew 'em that the astronauts landed on the moon and walked on the moon, and they were thrilled about that. They'd talk about their wives and their families, and I remember one time Joey said his wife told him about how a guy made a play for her when he was in the jail and Joey said he'd have to teach the guy not to do things like that.

They was religious, or at least their families were. They had a St. Christopher's medal on a magnetic base on their dashboard. And they'd wear crosses and medallions. They'd talk about how they'd have to take their wives or their children to a meeting at the church that night or about goin' to church on Sunday. They lived very, very normal lives except for the kind of work that they did. Somebody else goes off in the morning and kisses his wife and his kids goodbye and tells 'em he'll be back for dinner. Well, these guys do that too, only they're out casing a place for a robbery or stealing a car or hitting somebody.

Naturally they had a lot of interest in crime, and it seems like they were always discussing crimes, things they read in the papers, tryin' to figure out how it was done or what mistakes had been made. There was an attempted robbery at the Red Coach Inn in Boston then. Five men were involved. But the police had been tipped off about it and were waiting for 'em in unmarked cars in the parking lot and inside, in the restaurant. I think one or two of 'em escaped. The rest got captured. Well, Joey and Vince tried to visualize the thing. They tried to figure out how they all might have gotten out of it, why some got away and the others got captured.

They seemed to know a lot of criminals, to have a lot of contacts, especially Vince. He'd be talkin' to Joey about a party they went to the night before and say, "Did you see Frank there? He was one of 'em that did the First National Bank job two years ago." Or we'd be driving down a street, maybe in Boston, and Vince'd point to somebody and say, "That's Johnny, Arnold Carducci's bag man." It just seemed like he knew a lot of people and what they were doin' and what they had done and who worked for who. And they'd get tips about this job or that job. I figured they must've had some connection with the Mafia.

One time Vince called up and he says, "We got a job lined up." He sounded excited.

I said, "Well, good. What is it?"

He says, "It's a bank." He tells me how it's a little drive-in bank, the branch office of a big bank, and they had some information about when to take it and get some pretty good money. He said they'd cased it and it would be easy. And he said we were to meet the next day at one o'clock to work out the escape route and for me to see the bank. We did that, meeting at a shopping center that time, and they showed me the bank. They said that a lot of money is deposited there on paydays and stays there overnight until being sent on to the main office. We drove around lookin' for a route that couldn't be blocked by the police or by heavy traffic or by a train running across it, and we finally found one that suited us. They told me we'd do the job in five days, and we set up a time and a place to meet. And I thought, this is really something. I couldn't wait.

5

We had arranged to meet at a mall in Portsmouth. I had a .25 automatic. I'd take money from the restaurant to the bank or from the bank to the restaurant and I'd carry that automatic in my pocket in case of a robbery. That's why I had it. I put the gun in my coat pocket and waited outside on the sidewalk. It was dark. The days had been getting very short. Finally they drove up to where I was. "Let's go," I said.

They said, "It's off. Somethin's come up."

I said, "What? What're you talkin' about? What's goin' on?" You see, I was all set to do it and it was a letdown for me.

They said they had to help a friend, a cousin of Joey's. This guy had got busted and they had to get bail for him, a lawyer, one thing and another. That was their story. They said they promised the guy they'd help him and they promised the guy's family. In fact, it was Joey's family. They said they had to keep their word and we'd do the bank some other time. "Don't worry," they said. "We'll get it. Banks'll always wait."

We never did rob that bank. We'd keep talkin' about it as somethin' we had to do, but we never did get around to doin' it. I don't know, maybe they did do it eventually. Maybe they were just testing me, to see if I would inform on 'em. I thought about that, then, but I don't know.

I was gettin' very impatient now, because I had decided I was gonna do some crimes, and this waiting and planning and thinking about it was just making me jumpy and nervous. It was a month now since Joey and Vince had gotten out of jail, and all we had done was meet and talk and drive in their car and plan and scheme. I was getting tired of dropping quarters into the Hampton toll plaza.

The next Sunday one of 'em called me and said, "We got somethin' planned. Something big." He said I was to meet 'em at eleven that morning, at a certain mall. He said, "It's not the bank. It's somethin' else, possibly better. It's good. It's easy. We'll tell ya about it when we see ya."

I was sayin' to him, "Good. Good. Now you're talkin'." It surprised me that they wanted to do a robbery on a Sunday. I wouldn't've thought Sunday would be a good day for something like that, 'cause nothing would be open. But I didn't doubt that they knew what they were doin', and I got my gun like before, and I put it in my coat, told Donna that I had to go take care of some business for the band, line up a gig or somethin', and I hurried down to meet 'em.

It was in Massachusetts, at Haverhill. Vince said it'd be a cocktail bar or a lounge, and he said they were runnin' a bookie operation out of there. He said he had information that the money's picked up late Sunday, and so we'd be able to get all that plus whatever was in the cash register. And he said it should be pretty quiet in there, not too many customers, and the bartender would have no reason to protect the money since it wasn't his but belonged to the owner or whoever handled the booking operation.

I was worried that maybe the Mafia ran the booking operation, and I didn't want to mess with that. I didn't think the Mafia'd read me my rights and let me go consult with an attorney. And I said, "Is this thing connected?" I said, "Look, if this is the Mafia's money, I don't want any part of it. I don't want some guys to come gunnin' for me."

Vince says, "You don't have to worry about that. We'd know if there was anything like that and we wouldn't bother with it."

So I stopped worrying about that. For all I knew or know now, these guys were with the Mafia and had been directed to rob the place because it was competition. It didn't matter to me. All I wanted was to get started and to get my share. I figured this was it. And I was really nervous and excited all the way down there. There's nothin' like the thought of doin' an armed robbery to get the adrenalin goin'.

The bar didn't look like much. It was in a run-down, neglected part of the city. It was called the Scarlet Pub. I said, "It doesn't look to me like there'd be much money in there."

Vince said, "They don't usually hang a sign out sayin', 'Here's the money—come and get it.' "

We drove around it a couple times, and they explained they couldn't go in this time 'cause they'd be identified too easily, the bartender knew 'em. They had told me before they probably wouldn't be able to take many chances in that area. I knew that. They said, "You'll have to do this one alone."

I said, "Okay," I was as ready as I'd ever be. This was my chance. They were testing me.

They said, "Don't take any chances. Get out of there if you don't think you can do it."

I said, "Sure, sure." Then they showed me where they'd be waiting, around the block, and they drove around to the front of the place again and pulled over to the curb. I was in the front passenger seat, Vince was driving, and Joey was in the back seat. I says, "Well, I guess this is it." And I start to open the door.

Vince says, "Well, do you still want to go through with it?"

I says, "I've come this far, haven't I?"

He says, "That don't necessarily mean nothin'. A lot of guys've come this far."

I said, "I'm goin'. You just wait for me."

Then they shook my hand and said, "Good luck. Good luck, kid." They told me I had nothin' to worry about and that it would be easy as cake, and they drove off. I was standing at the curb with nothin' to do but open the door and go in. And I did that. It was dark in there, and I stood at the door while my eyes adjusted. There was a radio playin'. There was seven men in there. Six of 'em was customers and there was the bartender. They all looked like killers to me.

I walked up to the bar and I sat down. There was these people sittin' in a booth and one guy sittin' by himself at the bar and the bartender was wiping the counter. He came over to me and asked me what I wanted to drink. I ordered somethin', I can't remember what it was. I emptied the glass pretty quick too, because the next thing I knew the bartender was back, asking me if I wanted a refill. And I figured I had to do it now or never. I had the gun in my coat pocket, and I worked it out and had it lyin' in my hand on my lap. I said, "No, that isn't what I want. It's not a drink that I want." And I picked up the gun and laid it on the counter pointin' towards him with my finger on the trigger, and I said, "I think you know what I want." And I said, "This is a robbery. I don't plan on hurting anybody. Just go along with me and everything will be all right." I said, "I have information that you got a bookin' operation here and that you've got the money and it's not picked up yet. Well, I want it."

He says, "It's not here. It's already been picked up."

I picked up the gun off the counter and I pointed it at him and I said, "You're lyin'."

He says, "I'm not. If I had it, I'd give it to you. You can go lookin' for it if you don't believe me. There's no cash box or nothin' like that. Just what's in the cash register."

I looked behind the counter. I thought there might be a cigar box where money might be kept, something like that. There wasn't anything back there, and all this time I'm lookin' at the customers, lookin' at the door, lookin' at the bartender. I knew I had to do something. I didn't know what. Well, I got up off the stool. And I walked back until I was standin' in the middle of the room, and I shouted so they could all hear me, "This is a robbery. Just keep quiet and don't move and nobody'll get hurt." I said, "I don't want to hurt this man but I will if I have to." I had the gun pointed at the bartender at first, but while I was talkin' I swung it around and pointed it at this one and then at that one.

And I had a paper bag with me, and I threw it to the bartender, and I said, "Okay, empty out the cash register and give me that." He did that, and I kept lookin' around me and lookin' over at the door and swingin' my gun around and sayin' things like, "Don't nobody move" or "I got some friends outside coverin' for me, so don't give me any trouble."

The bartender emptied the cash register. There wasn't much in there. I told him to put his wallet in there. He said, "There's cards and things in there I want to keep. Let me have it. I'll give you the money." And I told him to just go along with what I said and he'd get his wallet back. Then I told the others to get up one after another and drop their wallets and jewelry into the bag. I pointed to 'em one after another with the gun. And all the time I kept lookin' around at the rest of 'em and the door. One guy tried to slip his wallet under his seat. I saw it out of the corner of my eye and turned real fast and pointed my gun at him. I shouted, "Pick up your wallet and put your hands on the table." It turned out that he had the most money of all of 'em, more than was in the register—about two hundred dollars and he tried to hide it from me.

I took the bag and got out of there. I backed up to the door and told 'em not to call the police or make any noise or anything for five minutes. They told the police I acted like a madman. They said I was screamin' the whole time and wavin' my gun all over. I don't know. Maybe I did. I suppose I was scared. They said they thought I was on drugs. They said I pistol-whipped 'em. I don't know why they said that. I definitely did not do that. I don't know why people have to make things worse than they are.

I ran down the alley, across a yard, and over a little fence, like I was supposed to, to get to the car. There they were. They were waitin' for me. They were really excited. They pushed open the door for me and they said, "Get in. Get in. Get in." And I jumped in and sank back in the side. And Vince pulled away, not drivin' too fast, so we wouldn't attract attention. And right away they wanted to know what it was like. I described it to 'em, and they couldn't believe that there was seven people in there and I went ahead and robbed the place anyway. They kept sayin', "You sure there was seven people in there?"

And I says, "Yes, six customers and the bartender."

And Vince says, "Well, you're okay. You've got the nerve that it takes."

I told them that the money we expected just wasn't there, the bartender said it had been already picked up, all I got was the money from the cash register and from the customers. It turned out to be about three hundred dollars. It wasn't big money. I said, "What happened? You said that would be a big haul."

Joey was furious. He started cussin', said he couldn't wait to get his hands on the guy that gave them the information. He was swearin' and cussin', sayin' he had expected a lot of money, but I was too relieved just to get out of there to be mad. I was disappointed, though. I thought it would be a big job. But Vince says, "Well, it's too bad we missed because that should have been good for over five thousand dollars. It'll be better next time." And he says, "But it was a good job, anyway. Any job that you come out of is a good job." That's the kind of influence that Vince had. He'd calm Joey down.

I told them those people were very concerned about their wallets, the cards and things, and I said, "I told the bartender I'd get the wallets back to them." Vince said he'd take care of it.

And I was pretty elated because I had done my first job. It was something I had never done before. I was on my way.

6

When they dropped me off that night, Vince said, "We'll keep in touch."

I said, "Sure. You bet."

He said, "Let us know if you need anything." Then he said, "Don't worry about it. We'll do better next time. We'll make a good one the next time."

Three days later, I believe it was a Thursday, I got a call from Joey. He said, "Come on down. We got some work." We agreed to meet in front of a post office.

I met them at the agreed time. There was Vince and Joey in the car, and another guy I had never seen before. They were really friendly, as they always were. "How you doin', Warren?" "Good to see you again." Then they introduced me to the other guy. They told me his name was Sammy.

Vince said, "Sammy, you won't believe this guy." He was talkin' about me. He said, "He's terrific. He's a natural. He did that job in the bar down in Haverhill I told you about. There was seven guys in there, *seven guys,* and he went ahead with the thing anyway. Jeez, I wouldn'ta done that. He's got a lot of balls. Balls like grapefruit. He's really a natural." Vince was carryin' on like that. I don't know if it was for my benefit or for Sammy's.

Vince said, "Warren, Sammy here's given us some information about a nightclub. He wants to participate in the robbery, take an active part in it, and get a percentage of the take. We told him that was okay with us. How do you feel?"

"Sure," I said. "That's fine."

I didn't drive that time. Joey drove. And there was a large nightclub, a very huge place. It was a restaurant as well as a drinking place. According to Sammy, they didn't deposit any money over the weekend. Thursday, Friday, and Saturday the money was there, and over Sunday. And they didn't go to the bank until Monday. We rode around and looked at it. It was a big place.

Vince said, "We're goin' to do it Sunday mornin'. That's when he makes his payroll, and he pays cash. The safe'll be open. There's very few people around." He said, "Warren, you and Sammy'll go in, and Joey and I'll wait in the car, with the guns. We'll cover you. Sammy already's got the hot box, and everything's all ready to go." He said I wouldn't be driving and so I wouldn't have to know the route or anything.

The plan was for Sammy to drive the car into the parking lot, next to the side door, with the motor running. We'd just go in and get the payroll and leave with the receipts. We'd meet Joey and Vince further down the road, and then we'd abandon the stolen car and drive off with them.

Vince said to me on the way back to our meeting point that night, "You know, Warren, we'd like to go in. Joey and I would really like to go in. But we're so well known that we're easily identified." What he said made sense, and it's probably true. I guess they'd been in so much trouble around in those areas that the police had a pretty good work-up on them.

So I went down Sunday morning as was planned. We met in a side street, an apartment parking lot, down where they lived. We locked the cars and picked up the stolen car and made the final plans. Joey and Vince were to cruise back and forth down the highway, and if there was any trouble they was to come in from behind and straighten the trouble out.

I got in the stolen car with Sammy and we drove down to the nightclub. Sammy pulled into the parking lot, over by the door, just like he was supposed to. I had my hand on the car door, just startin' to get out of the car, and Sammy said, "Oh, Jesus!" I thought there was cops all around us the way he said it. He said, "We can't do it. We just can't do it." He was almost shaking.

I said, "What are you talking about?" I said, "Everything's all ready to go."

He said, "I know that guy that just walked into the place. That's the bartender. He's there. He knows me. He knows me. I can't do it." And he screamed out of that parking lot. The tires was smoking. And the guy's lookin' at him like he's some kind of a fool. Sammy was bent over the wheel, all stiff and tight, rushing to get out of there. So we never did do that one.

Joey and Vince were angry. They were very much upset. They said, "What happened?" Sammy told 'em. Joey said, "It don't make no damn difference. We ought to go back." But Sammy wouldn't do it. He was all broke up.

Vince said, "It don't make no difference who's there. There's always gonna be people around." They was yellin' at Sammy, chewin' him out. They was a little bit upset because the robbery wasn't goin' to take place.

Finally, though, they dumped the hot box. Sammy wanted to keep it and do a job later that night by himself. They wouldn't let him. They said, "We've had it too long. They're goin' to be lookin' for it. The hell with you, we're gonna dump the thing." So they made Sammy dump it, and we all got in their car and drove off. We dropped Sammy off in some city somewhere, I don't remember.

And they was grumblin' after they let him off. Joey said, "What a jerk that guy is."

And Vince said, "We won't listen to him again." And Vince said Sammy couldn't go on no more jobs with them.

I said, "We don't seem to be gettin' much done. We talked about bein' busy. We talked about scores. We talked about big money." I said, "We've had one flop and two that we didn't even touch. Is it always gonna be like this?"

Vince said, "Oh, no, no, this is just weird. I've never seen nothin' like it before."

I said, "Well, I hope so, 'cause the risk is still the same." I said, "The penalty is still the same if you come out with a dollar or a hundred thousand dollars."

We had a rap about that. They said, "Don't worry, we'll get into it. We'll get into the good stuff. Just keep gettin' out of them the way you do and you'll be all right. And don't worry about gettin' grabbed. If you get grabbed you won't be in too much trouble, because you've never been arrested before, and we'll come down with the money and make sure you get a good lawyer and a bail bondsman, and you'll be right out, so don't let that worry you."

I said, "It's not worryin' me. I don't plan on bein' caught."

7

A supper club was the next one. They called me down. Joey called, said, "We got a good one this time."

I said, "When is it?"

He said, "Right now. We can do it easy. It's a piece of cake." That's what they called 'em. Somethin' they thought was easy was a piece of cake. I think they saw it on TV.

So I come down and we went over to the supper club. They're drivin'. We don't even have a stolen car this time. This was another deal like the first one, where I was supposed to come out the door and go down the alley and across to the next block where the people there couldn't see the car. So I asked 'em what that was.

Vince said, "Well, it's not a great amount of money but we ought to come out with a couple grand apiece. We figure there's probably five, six thousand dollars in there."

I don't know why they would have thought that. It was a small place. If I was walkin' down the street, lookin' for a place to rob, I'd go right by there. And the only reason I went in is because they said this'd probably be good.

It was the early evening, probably four-thirty or five in the evening. I went into the club, and there was a man and a woman sittin' at the bar. And they were way down at the end, and they were juke-boxing, sittin' there.

I had a paper bag with me, and my gun. I sat at the bar and the owner came over. I ordered a drink while I just looked the place over to see if there was any people out back. I was tryin' to get an idea of the place. I finished the drink and the owner came over again and asked me if I wanted another one. I said, "No, but I'll take all the money." And I showed him the gun. Then I gave him the bag.

The guy and the girl down the bar didn't even look up. They quit talkin' and they didn't say a word and they just kept their heads right straight aforward. They didn't even want to see me. They knew what was goin' on. They just sat right there.

The bartender says, "Okay, okay, no problem." He said, "There ain't much here. All I got's the bank from the night's business."

I said, "I don't want to hear it, just put the money in." I said, "You got anything out back? You got anything stashed? You got a safe?" And I looked around. I didn't see anything that looked like a cash box. I raised up, you know, and I looked down on the counters underneath the cash register, and I didn't see anything. And I didn't know how much money was there. It looked like a decent amount of bills. I said, "Just dump everything in there."

I left. And on the way out, I pulled the phone. I said, "Don't follow me. No, don't try to follow me."

He said, "Oh, no, no. I won't do anything. I'll just do what you say."

I said, "Well, just stay in here five minutes. That's all." I said, "Just don't try to follow me." I asked him if that was the only phone.

He says, "Yes."

I said, "Are you sure you don't have a safe?"

He said, "No. No, that's all the money. You got it all." So I left.

Joey said, "How'd you do, kid?"

I said, "Good. Good. I had no problems. Right in and out."

He said, "Tell me about it. Who was there?" I described the guy. He said, "Yeh, that's the owner." I guess he knew him. He said, "Did you get the money?"

I said, "Yeah, it's in the bag. I got everything he had.

He said, "Well, let me see it. Was anybody else there?"

I told him about the guy and the girl. And he laughed about that 'cause the guy didn't look up. He said, "He's probably a crook himself. That's why he knew better than to look at you."

Vince was drivin'. Joey counted the money. He said, "I don't believe it." He said, "That's all he gave you?"

I said, "Yeah." I said, "There's the bag. I just come right out with it, jumped in the car. Where the hell you think I'd put it? That's all."

He said, "There's nothing here. Just a lousy couple hundred bucks. That was supposed to be a five-grand hit. That score was supposed to be worth five thousand dollars."

I said, "I don't know who's givin' you your information, but somethin's wrong." I said, "You're gettin' bum information or we're hittin' it wrong or we're doin' somethin'. 'Cause each time it's like this."

He said, "Well, we ain't gonna get a big one every time. But I figured this time we'd each get a buck, buck and a half, apiece."

I said, "Well, he didn't have it, and I don't think he was lyin'."

He said, "Did you take him out back and look for a safe?"

I said, "No, I didn't take him out back and look for no safe. I ain't goin' out there, out back, and leave that customer out there. I don't care if he had a safe full of money. You didn't tell me there was no safe. I just done what you said and where the money was supposed to be."

He said, "I'll bet it's in the safe. I'll bet there's a safe there and we missed it."

I said, "All right, maybe so. If you had told me that, I'd have got it. But I don't think there's any safe." I told them, "I want to get in on something good. I don't care what it is. If we're gonna do it, we might as well go for some money."

Vince said, "Well, we agree. Both of these was supposed to be good. And them other ones. Too bad we missed that nightclub. That would have been some big money. Too bad we didn't get that bank. That would have been good. We'd have been fat now."

This was coming into the fall of the year. Vince said, "Look, we'll get some good scores between now and Christmas. Then we'll ease up. And after Christmas, I tell you, we'll have all kinds of money. And we'll all go to Bermuda, take the families, for a vacation."

I said, "All right."

8

The next one was a market. It was supposed to be a bookie station, but it was a market. It was in a marketplace in Boston, a little Italian guy had it.

Vince was gonna circle. And Joey went over in a bakery store window to watch me from across the street. I could see his eyes peekin' out the window. Silly lookin'. I didn't laugh, 'cause I figured he didn't know how stupid he looked, peekin' out that window. And he kept bouncin' up and down. And he kept stretchin' his neck, and his eyes looked like they was balls, lookin' out the window.

So I went in the market. It was mornin'. And there was this guy, real Italian guy. He even talked like this—whats-a this and whats-a that. Real accent. And he had on an athletic shirt, with a great big belly, and a black pair of pants. His belly hung way out over his belt. His athletic shirt was dirty. He wasn't clean-shaven. He was an ornery cuss, a wise guy.

I was lookin' around. There wasn't any customers in there. I was watchin' the door, and I went over to look at some things. I asked if he had, I don't know, some foolish thing.

"Nah, I don't got that." He's growlin'. He was a strange kind of person to be in business. Until I stepped around the corner and put the gun on him, and then he melted right there. He changed his whole attitude. He got sweet. He got real sweet. I said, "All right, wise mouth."

He said, "No, no, no, no."

I said, "Don't make any funny moves. You know what I'm here for." I said, "You're in the business. Get the money out."

He said, "No. No, no, no, no." He said, "What are you-a doin' this to me for? I'm-a one of you. I'm-a one of you guys." And he's layin' a rap.

I said, "I don't want to hear your rap." I said, "I want the money."

He said, "The money ain't here. It ain't here. You're early."

I said, "Look, you're supposed to have five thousand dollars. I ain't gonna screw around with you. You're supposed to have five thousand dollars. You're carryin' it today. For the book. And you're gonna get off it."

He said, "No, no, don't shoot me."

I said, "I ain't gonna shoot you. I ain't gonna do nothing. Either you're gonna get the money or I'm leavin', and I'm gonna send somebody else back and beat your head in. How's that?" And I said, "You ain't gotta be worried about this gun, 'cause I ain't gonna shoot you unless you do somethin' stupid like tryin' to jump me. I ain't gonna shoot you if I don't get the money. I'm gonna send them guys back, and that's worse. You'd rather I shoot ya." I said, "I'm leavin'."

He said, "Wait. Wait, wait, wait. What are you-a doin' this to me for? I'm-a one of you guys."

I said, "I don't know what you are. I was sent here."

He says, "Look, there ain't no payoff money here. It's not here."

I said, "If you're lyin', they'll know you're lyin'. I'm gonna tell 'em what you said." I said, "What have you got in the cash register?"

He had some change in there. I got mad. I said, "Stick it." I said, "Give me your wallet."

He said, "I need them papers. I need the photographs. What do they matter to-a you?"

I said, "You'll get it back. Unless you're lyin', and then you won't need it. If you're lyin', you won't need the wallet. You'll be in the hospital for a while." I said, "I think you're lyin'."

He said, "I swear I ain't lyin'. I ain't lyin'. I'll-a tell you-a what I'll do. You think I'm-a lyin', huh?" He says, "I know where there is some money. Down the street, so-and-so." And he said some name.

I said, "I don't know the guy."

He said, "It don't make no difference. He's carryin' the book. And I know he's got the money on him right now. And I know it is five thousand dollars. You go and get your guys, and you-a go and-a get him, and come back and give me 10 percent."

I said, "Yeah, I'll do that for sure. Thanks for the tip."

He said, "You're pretty good, man. You're pretty good at

this." As I went out the door, he said, "Don't forget to bring me back the 10 percent." He was talkin' like a buddy.

There was seven dollars in the wallet. Joey almost went insane. And I was furious. I was really furious. So Vince said, "That's okay, that's okay. We'll get another one this afternoon. We'll get him later. We'll get him."

Joey was so mad he couldn't even see straight. He wanted to go in there and punch him all over the place. Vince said, "Look, these things happen. It ain't anyone's fault. It ain't the guy's fault. For sure, it's our fault for not checking it out better. What're you mad about?"

Joey said, "I'm gettin' sick of this nickel-and-dime stuff."

Vince said, "Well, cool off. Beatin' the guy won't do any good. We'll just wait and get him later when he is carryin' somethin'. We know he carries."

Joey said, "He's got the money in there. I know he does. He's slippery."

I said, "Well, maybe so, but what do you want me to do, go through all the shelves in the store? I told him if he didn't get it up that you guys'd hunt him down, you guys'd come down and needle him."

Vince said, "Well, that's good. Then he'd have given it to you if he'd've had it. Anyway, we've got this other thing this afternoon that we can do. And that should be pretty good pickin's up there."

9

After that stupid thing at the market, we drove around rapping, had something to eat. They talked about what they had in mind for the afternoon. It was a jewelry outfit. And the way they talked you'd think there were diamond mines. This guy was supposed to be loaded, really loaded. All kinds of art work in his home, collections—they really laid it on. I thought, "Well, this is gonna be a million-dollar heist."

The friggin' place is in a great big buildin' in Lowell. It's up on maybe the twelfth floor. And it's a dinky one-man operation, and it's right over the sheriff's office.

Well, they parked on the other side of a commons. Vince says, "This won't take you long and it oughta be a good score. We oughta get a nice piece of change out of this."

So I goes up. I walked up the stairs. And I sees this county sheriff's office and I think, what the hell is a sheriff's office doin' here? I didn't think anyone was there, but I didn't know. And I kept thinkin' about it in the back of my mind the whole time.

And I went in and I looked around, and this guy didn't have much on display there.

I said to the guy, "I'm here to rob you." I didn't even take my gun out. I told him I had a gun. I says, "Just don't pull anything funny and you won't get hurt. I'm just after the money. Some people sent me down and they said you had diamonds and cash here, and I'm to pick it up and rob you."

He started laughin'. He says, "Who sent you?"

I says to myself, "Another one." Cause he's laughin'. The guy laughed.

He says, "Who sent you?"

I says, "It don't matter who sent me."

He says, "Well, they sure don't know much, robbin' me." He says, "I don't have nothin'. If you took the whole place, it wouldn't be worth your time."

And I looked around, and I think the most expensive watch he had on display was $29.95. There wasn't any Omega watches. There wasn't any Benrus. There wasn't anything high priced or solid gold or nothing, in the place. And I was mad, I was really mad. I was so mad, I didn't take nothin'. I didn't rob him, I didn't do nothin'.

I says, "I think you're tellin' me the truth."

He says, "I am tellin' you the truth. Whoever sent you, don't know what the hell they're doin'. You know what this is? I'm retired." He says, "This is a hobby with me. I got a few customers, and they like little trinkets and things for gifts and stuff." He says, "I don't have any high-priced customers and things like that."

106

I says, "Keep it. Just keep it." And I got out of there. I thought the guy would press the alarm, so after I got past the sheriff's office I hurried. But the door I planned to use was locked and barred. I thought, "Jesus, this is it." I had to walk all the way around the building to find a door.

I got to the car and I says, "This one was the worst of all. The guy didn't have nothin'. And I'm not gonna go on like this no more. If you don't come up with somethin', then I will on my own. I don't want to do no more jobs like these, just come up with nothin', or fifty or a hundred dollars. That's ridiculous. Kids get more than that out of candy stores."

Vince said, "Don't do that. Don't go off. We'll come up with somethin'." They wanted to know if there was anythin' up my way.

I says, "Yeah, there might be. I'll look around."

He says, "Okay, don't do anything foolish. Don't do anything until you hear from us. And we'll get somethin' goin'."

10

Saturday, Joey called me up. He wanted to know if I was doin' anything. He wanted to come up. Could I meet him somewhere? Did I know Exeter?

I said, "Sure I do."

He said, "Okay, can you meet me over there?"

I said, "Yeah, I'll meet you in the parking lot, near the town hall."

I was late. I was having trouble with my car. When I got there, he says, "Where you been? Where you been?" They didn't like me to be late, or anybody to be late. I told him I was havin' trouble with my car. And he says, "Well, you got to get it fixed. That's bad. You'll get stranded on the highway. Someday you'll need to count on it. You don't want it to let you down."

I said, "What do you want?"

He said, "Well, let's take a ride. Hop in. Leave your car here."

He says, "I think we can do one this afternoon." He says, "It's gettin' late in the season. We gotta get movin'. We've been goofin' off long enough. We gotta start movin'."

I says, "All right."

We drove through Haverhill, Massachusetts, out to Western Products. He says, "Here's the place. I've got some information on it. We was gonna do it later, but we need the loot and we're behind schedule and things ain't been turnin' out right." He says, "They got a payroll. They pay today. They pay cash."

I said, "Are you serious?"

He says, "Yeah, they do."

I said, "Well, we're gonna get that."

So I went in and I looked the place over. There was a couple of people there, and a woman asked if she could help me. She was sittin' at a desk. All the main offices was upstairs, and she was sittin' in the reception area, with a phone. She's doin' the payroll. There was other people there, and I didn't want to get involved with them. So I told her I wanted an application for work.

I walked out. I went to the car. Joey was waitin', he said everything seemed to be good. He said, "Did you get it?"

I said, "No. No. I got an application."

He said, "Well, why?"

I said, "There was some people there. They came in."

He says, "Well, how does it look?"

I said, "The money's sittin' right on the desk top."

"Are you *serious!*" He's goin' crazy now, he's gettin' all excited.

I says, "I'm tellin' you, I've never seen nothin' like it. Her desk is covered with pay envelopes. The whole top is covered, and she's the only one there when them people leave."

He almost went off the road, he was so excited. So he spun around, we saw the people leave. He pulled in the parking lot, drove off, and I walked in again.

She says, "What do you want?"

I says, "I don't want nothin'. I don't want no noise out of you or nothin'. This is a holdup."

And she started screamin', yellin' at the top of her lungs. She says, "No, you're not gettin' the money. He's robbin' us! He's robbin' us!" And a whole bunch of people start runnin' downstairs from the offices upstairs above us.

I held the gun up and told 'em to get back. And they ran back, out of sight, out of my vision, up the stairwell. And the boss or somebody yelled down, "Give him the money. Just give him the money."

She says, "I will not!"

I says, "Don't be stupid, lady." I guess she went into shock or somethin' 'cause here I am standing with a gun. She don't know if I'm a drug addict, she don't know if I'm a killer, she don't know what. She's actin' real stupid. She could get herself shot doin' that.

So I starts takin' the money off the top of the desk. I says, "Just shut up."

She starts fightin' me, grabbin' me, scratchin' my hands, clawin' on me. And the money's flyin' all over the floor. I'm sweepin' what I can in the bag I got, and I says, "You're crazy." And she kept gettin' braver 'cause I didn't do nothin' when she attacked me.

When I was pickin' up the money on the corner of the desk top, I saw the cash box lyin' in an open drawer. And I reached down to get that, and she kicked the drawer closed on my hand. Yeah, she did, squashed my hand. I pulled it out, said, "You're weird." Crazy bitch.

So I just settled for what I had and took off. It was either that or hit her or shoot her or somethin'. I couldn't put up with her no longer, she was gettin' ready to jump on my back. That's all I gotta be doin', wrastlin' her, and have somebody come in the door after their pay and there'd be two of 'em.

She was a vicious, vicious person. She is dangerous. She is. She's a threat to society more than I am. If people knew what she was like, they'd have her investigated.

I ran out. I said, "That's it." The money was spread all over the floor, it was wiped off the desk top, but I had quite a few pay envelopes. I got out while the gettin' was good. I knew that she was flippin' right out. She knew I wasn't gonna hurt her. She knew that after the first few times, 'cause I would have slapped her or somethin', knocked her on the floor or back in the chair. Yeah, that would have probably ended her. But I never, just never intended to use that gun to hurt people, or to hurt people in any way. I just couldn't, any more than I could rob somebody that was poor. I guess I did rob some people that was poor, but I was told that they had all kinds of money, that they had bookie money, that they had this, that they had that. Like when I was robbin' that payroll, I knew that the company was obligated for that. I wasn't stealin' off the working man. They gotta give them their weekly salary. You don't get out of paying a man his salary just 'cause you got robbed.

I got back to the car and we drove off. Joey said, "How d'you do?"

I said, "Oh, man, you won't believe it."

He said, "Didn't you get it?"

I said, "I got it. I got it. Just keep goin'. Let me rest, calm down." So I ducked down in the seat in case she had given a description and the cops were lookin' for me. I said, "I'm gonna jump in the back and lay down." I said, "Just drive, will ya?"

He said, "Okay, okay. Good boy."

So I jumped in the back and lay down on the seat. I was angry and excited, scared, and, you know, everything. But I calmed down.

He says, "It looks pretty good." He had opened the bag. He says, "You got quite a bit there."

I said, "I don't know if I do or not."

He said, "What happened, anyway?"

I said, "I told her it's gonna be a robbery. I told her no one's gonna be hurt, I just wanted the money. I wasn't there to hurt anybody. And she started screamin' and hollerin', 'He's robbin' me! He's robbin' me!' And people comin' down the stairs."

He says, "No kiddin'?"

I says, "Yeah."

He says, "I heard of stuff like that before, women doin' stuff like that." He says, "Go on. Tell me about it."

So I told him what happened. He starts laughin'. He says, "Too bad." He says, "Not too much money fell on the floor, did it?"

I says, "I don't know, and I don't care. She was gettin' ready to jump right up on my shoulders and pick my eyes out."

He says, "I once heard a story of a robbery at a supermarket. A couple of guys were involved in it. One of 'em is standing by the door, with a submachine gun or somethin', and a woman comes in. So he points the gun at her and tells her to get into a phone booth which was there. Then he closes the door on her. Well, he's waitin' for his buddy to come with the money, and he hears the sound of a dial turnin'. She's standin' in that phone booth, practically right next to him, callin' the police." He says, "That's why, if you ask any robber, he'll tell you, 'Don't ever hold up a woman.' They just aren't afraid of bein' hurt like a man would be."

I says, "Now you tell me."

We didn't come out of that one poor. There was twelve or fifteen hundred dollars in that robbery. And he was tickled. He says, "Vince gets his part, right?" He says, "We always was partners."

I says, "Sure. I feel that way about it."

He says, "Yeah, well, that'll make Vince feel good if you feel that way."

Well, we split the money up. Each of us got about four hundred dollars. And I felt pretty good 'cause that was a pretty solid piece of spendin' money. I figured I finally did somethin' that did amount to somethin' in the way of a robbery.

11

The next time, Joey came alone again, and he said, "This time it's gonna be a bank." It was December 12th or 15th, I think.

I said, "Where's it at?"

He says, "Right over here. I'm gonna drive by it now."

It was in Epping. The Epping Bank. It's a tiny town, the main highway goes right by it. I had played music in Epping, jam sessions.

He drove through the town and I said, "A bank, huh?" I hadn't done a bank before. And I always thought there's always money in every bank. I just figured that a bank was the place to rob, which isn't so. But I thought that at the time, and I was pretty excited. I was gonna get some money. It was pretty foolish messin' around with somethin' like that, so close to home. But I didn't think of that, either, at the time. I just didn't think of gettin' caught. I didn't plan on gettin' caught, and I didn't even think I would.

So he says, "Look at that. There's the bank." And it was a real old thing. It looked like somethin' out of a western movie, the bank is so old. He said, "There's an owner or manager that's sometimes in the bank and, at the most, a teller." He says, "There won't be nothing to it. You can handle it very easy." He says, "What do you say we do it?"

I said, "All right."

I went in alone. Joey waited in the car, near the place. There was only one person there, a lady. The bank was very old and I didn't know where anything was, so I told her I wanted some change, a roll of quarters, and she said, "I'll have to go out back and get that." And she went out back where the safe was, and she came back.

And I said, "Okay. This is a holdup." I showed her the gun, I leaned over the counter. I said, "Just come back here and sit down." And I went back and emptied the safe, and then I emptied the front cash drawers. Another person came in, and I didn't let that person know there was a robbery in progress. I guess she thought I worked there or was a delivery man or somethin'. She didn't pay much attention to me, didn't even hardly look at me. I said to her, "The lady would like to see you out back, back in the office."

She said, "Oh, all right, thank you."

I held the gateway for her to go through. And she went back, and I finished emptyin' the cash drawers out front, and by then she knew it was a robbery.

I told them, "Just stay there for five minutes." And I threatened them, you know, sounding tough. "There's people outside, one of 'em's got a machine gun." The whole bit, you know. I said, "You don't want to be shot up. It's comin' Christmas time and you want to be with your kids. Let the insurance worry about this money. Don't risk your life for it." And I left.

We got out of there. Joey said, "We gotta get hold of Vince. He'll be tickled when he hears about this." So we stopped and Joey called him. He told him we were going to pick him up, that we got the money and it was a good job. Vince was all excited.

We picked up Vince and drove to a friend or maybe a relative's house of theirs. We counted out the money. It was good, about six thousand dollars. We divided it up. They gave me, along with my share, the Canadian bills, the odd change, and things like that. They said we should give some money to the guy whose house we was using. They said we should give him some money for letting us use his place to count up the money. They told me he needed some money pretty bad anyway. I said, "Sure."

The money was there. The job was completed. And they were really excited. Vince said, "Hey, you're doin' all the work. You're doin' good. But we'll get into some big stuff. We'll do our part. We know you're doin' all the work. You're the one that's always goin' in. But we got some stuff comin' up out of state. We'll take an active part. You can lay back for a little bit. We'll make it right with you." They said, "You're a champ, you're really beautiful," and all that stuff. And I was pretty pleased to get the money.

They had a meal cooked up and I ate. They wanted to go celebrate and I told them, "I don't mess around much that way." I said, "I gotta get back." I didn't feel much like celebratin'.

They said, "Sure. Sure. Anything you want. Everything's fine. And you know you're welcome any time. We're gonna throw a party sometime that'll amaze you."

So I left. I had about eighteen or nineteen hundred dollars.

When we were counting the money, Joey found a deposit slip for twenty-five thousand dollars for the parent bank in Exeter. The slip was dated the day before the robbery. If we had hit it one day sooner, we'd have gotten more than thirty thousand.

12

We hit a slack period after that. We went and looked at a couple of things and they didn't prove out. Things didn't work. For a period of a few days, anyway, it went dull. It was Christmas time and I took a trip with the family to New York, to visit relatives. They had said that we'd cool it and then after Christmas do a couple of big ones and then lay low for a while. One of the newspapers down there had printed a warning to someone they called the phantom robber. That was me. The newspaper said, "We predict that if you keep it up you'll be dead or in prison within six months." I didn't know it, but the police had a shoot-on-sight on me.

It sounds crazy now, but I didn't know, for example, that I could get shot. I always pictured police detective work and maybe someone sayin', "Okay, you're wanted for arrest," or someone knockin' on the door and sayin', "We got a warrant for you." I just never thought of bein' shot down in the street and not given a chance to surrender or be taken into custody. I think the thing was I just didn't visualize my being a danger to anyone else or the guys I was with shooting somebody. Even if they had ran over somebody with a car, gettin' away, it would have been murder one, 'cause it would happen in the commission of a felony. Even if somebody had ran a stop light and hit us. I know those things now. But strange as it seems, I didn't take all those things into consideration. Things were developin' so fast, I probably didn't take the time to sit and think and realize the potential for violence that was there, the impact there would be, if I was caught, on my life and on everybody else's—my family, my friends, the band. It seems like the actions of a real thoughtless, selfish, careless person. And they would have been if I had known all the danger in these things and just went ahead with them anyway. But I didn't speculate on it at all. I just thought I'd never get caught and I'd quit when I got the amount of money I wanted.

I'd have quit at eighty or a hundred thousand dollars and, really, I done enough work and I took enough risks to get that much. You see, I had some things that I wanted to get done. I knew that I was gonna hafta hire counsel, here in New Hamp-

114

shire and in California, to keep my sons from bein' sent back to California through the efforts of a social worker out there. The social worker was interested in the rehabilitation of their mother. He wasn't interested in the boys' welfare, but I was. That would have cost thousands of dollars, and that's one of the reasons for the high figure. I had visions of maybe outfittin' the band properly with clothing and equipment and gettin' a good booking agent and puttin' the band on the road. And I was lookin' further ahead to real estate in some part of the country where I'd want to settle down in, a ranch-type place, invest in that. So I figured that eighty or a hundred thousand dollars was all I needed for working capital for the things that I felt I wanted to get done at the time. And I didn't see any honest way of comin' by that money.

It was at this time that I introduced my family to my religion. I saw two elders on the street one day. Whenever I see two Mormon elders walkin', I know exactly who they are. I don't know how. It isn't that they dress peculiar. They're not dressed up in robes or a bead on their forehead. No, they're dressed up in suits. But I can spot Mormon elders anywhere. I don't know why this is. But I saw them, and they were tracting, out on their mission. They don't stand on the corner and throw pieces of paper at people, like some of the religions do. They go door-to-door and introduce themselves and say they have a message about God and ask people if they'd be willin' to listen.

I stopped them on the street and I asked 'em if they were Mormons. And they said, "Yes, we are."

And I said, "You are the elders in your mission?"

And they said, "Yes."

And I asked 'em to go to my house. In fact, I took 'em home with me and I introduced 'em to Donna and the family. And I told the family that they were missionaries from my church and they had a message and I felt like it would help them if they listened to it and I'd like them to listen to it. Maybe out of respect for me or whatever, Donna said that she would be willing to, and the boys were, too. So they were given their lesson in the home. They were prepared, and they embraced the faith and became baptized.

115

You see, I knew I was doin' wrong and I still felt that that was right. It may be all right for me to go to hell, but I don't want my kids goin' there. It's not a double standard, either. It's genuine concern. I wasn't carin' about myself before. Unselfishness isn't always a virtue. Quite often it's a virtue to be selfish.

13

Between Christmas and New Year's 1969, I called Joey to let him know I got back from vacation.

He said, "Well, if you're not doin' anythin', why don't you come down? We haven't seen you for a while." We had become pretty good friends. I felt like I could rely on them, and even though we hadn't known each other for a very long time, there was a lot of trust. Has to be.

I went down to talk to him, and he said he thought we might do one more big one and get a lot of money. He told me he and Vince had discussed maybe all of us gettin' our families together and goin' to Bermuda for a few weeks in January. And I liked the thought of doin' that. You know, things had been tough. Gettin' the boys from California, movin' up here from Nashville, settin' up the band—all that had been tough. It had taken a lot of money. Things had been nip and tuck. My parents and anyone that could help me contributed money. But things had been pretty rough. And it had been rough for Donna. I thought it would be nice to take her and the kids to Bermuda, with Vince and Joey and their families, for a couple of weeks. It would kinda make things up to her.

So I consented to do another robbery, which I would've done probably anyway, though I did feel we was being probably too active, and we had drawn a lot of attention to ourselves.

We rode around and looked at several places—small banks. We saw one that Joey liked the looks of in Merrimack, Massachusetts. It's a little town on the New Hampshire line, on the outskirts of Haverhill, Massachusetts. We zeroed in on that one and checked it out for several days. We cased it and got as much information as we could. The manager or owner had a habit pattern, we found out. Like every day he'd go to lunch at a certain time and stay gone for a certain length of time, which was good for us. There was only two other employees in there while he was gone. They were female employees. And there was only, I think, one police cruiser in town.

Vince for some reason wasn't available at that time, and Joey felt like I shouldn't go in alone, I should have somebody with me. He says, "You always should, really. Especially in a bank." He says, "Try to get somebody to go."

I told him I didn't know anybody I could depend on, and I didn't, in fact, find anybody. He had some people he thought would come in. They kept fallin' through, makin' excuses, one thing and another. They'd say they'd make it and then the last minute they couldn't make it.

He was gettin' fed up and I was too. I was gettin' very angry at the delay 'cause I felt that we had cased the thing enough. And I didn't want a repeat of what had happened at the other bank where they made a large deposit. So I called Joey finally and asked to meet him. I told him I was ready if he was and that I'd go it alone. Joey did find somebody to drive the good car and he left him stationed several miles away from the bank. And he was gonna wait or drive around the town in the stolen car.

So we drove down to the town of Merrimack. Joey and I checked to see if the good car was stationed right. Then we went over to the bank. Joey said, "Don't stay too long. Get right out." They didn't like to stay in a bank more than three minutes. Then he drove off. We was to meet about two blocks away.

So I went in. It's like an old-fashioned bank you can see in a western movie. The counters was high. There were bars like you see in the windows of a prison, clean up to the ceiling. From the floor to the ceiling it was barred, like prison bars. And the windows were like prison cell windows, with just an open space in the bottom for transacting business in the bank. The rest of it was all barred. It was like a fort type of thing, just like in a western movie. It was a very old bank.

There was only two elderly ladies working there, so far as I could see. They had white hair. They kind of reminded me of my grandmother. This was the time of day when the guy who owned or managed the place was gone. And we had created a diversion to get the police out of town. Or Joey did. He called the police and told them he was a resident about six miles out of town. He said he had been hearin' a lot of shooting and wanted them to check on it. So the police left. The town had no police. I didn't figure on havin' any trouble. I figured I would be out of there in five minutes, if that long.

I had two shopping bags with me, paper shopping bags. And I put one on the counter. And the two ladies was sittin' at the desks. They hadn't even got up to wait on me. It was that fast. I told 'em, I says, "This is a robbery." I says, "Don't get nervous. Don't panic. And don't press no alarms. Nobody's gonna get hurt. I'm just here for the money. That's all I want. And as soon as I get the money I'll leave. And the more you cooperate, the faster I'll be gone." I was talkin' to them like that.

They said they didn't want to get hurt and they'd give me the money. I said, "That's all I want." So the first lady did, and then she went and sat down. It seemed like they didn't even bother to look at me very much. I found out afterwards that one of 'em was the wife of the ex-police chief of the town, and I guess he had schooled her, instructed her in those kind of things. But, for whatever reason, the ladies were very calm during the robbery.

I went to the second window, had the lady come over. I gave her a second bag. Now, the second window must have been set up for a different kind of business or a big business or somethin', because there was big bills there. In the first window I didn't notice any twenties or fifties, just small bills, but in the second window I did notice large-denomination bills and a large number of 'em. Quite a few. In fact, that's what caused me the trouble. The bag filled right up. She had to stuff the bag. It was a shopping bag full of large-denomination bills. And she started to slide the thing under the window. It was not a very big openin' and the bag jammed in it. I'm holdin' the money that I got from the first window under my arm, I had my gun in my right hand, and I was pullin' on the bag she had, tryin' to get it out from the window. I says, "Give it to me. Give it to me," 'cause I had been in the bank too long now. I says, "Hurry it up."

She says, "I'm goin' as fast as I can. Don't be nervous."

And we're rappin' back and forth like that. I am gettin' nervous, I'm gettin' *very* nervous, 'cause I had been in there a long time. And I said, "Give it to me." She's pushin' on the bag and I'm pullin' on it. And I had the gun in my hand, and I'm tryin' to get the bag out of there but it's stuck, there's too much money in the thing. And I'm sayin', "Give it to me."

And I heard a man's voice say, "I'll give it to you." And he's not supposed to be there. There's not supposed to be a man anywhere around.

And I just froze. It seemed like I froze. I got a prickly feeling, like people say your hair raises up. Well, it doesn't. But you get that feeling. A cold chill. Tingles. 'Cause somethin's wrong, you know. That male voice.

I looked up and I couldn't have clear vision of him 'cause I was lookin' at an angle. He was way to my right. But I looked up and there was this man standin' there broadside, and he's got a gun, and he's levelin' it right at my head, right at the side of my head. This pistol. Maybe twelve or fifteen feet away. Couldn't miss at that range. He was the owner or the manager of that bank. And he was pullin' the gun out of a holster on his side when he said, "I'll give it to you." And I looked up and the gun was being pulled right down at the side of my head. He didn't say, "Stop or I'll shoot." He didn't say, "Freeze." He didn't say no more. He just said, "I'll give it to you." And that's exactly what he was doin'.

I saw the gun. I threw my arm up, not aiming the gun at him, just sort of a ducking, reflex motion, and I turned my head. I thought I was dead. I threw my gun up and it was covering the side of my head, my hand was.

The gun went off and the bullet went through my finger and into the stock of my gun. A miracle saved me. He was aimin' for the side of my head and he's a marksman. He shoots with the police out on the range all the time. If I hadn't reflexed just like that, if I hadn't turned my head and put my hand up like wardin' off a blow, I'da been dead. The bullet woulda smacked me just above the ear.

I dropped down below the counter. It was a high counter, way above the waist. Not like the modern banks, with the low counters. I left the bag stuck under the window.

I don't know what he thought, but one of the women said, "Oh, my God," and it sounded like she was faintin'. It seemed like she was sayin' that as the air was comin' out of her lungs. And I think that she really thought that I had been shot dead and that she had witnessed a pretty bad thing. But I wasn't thinkin' about her much right then, 'cause that gun was the loudest thing I ever heard. It seemed like it went off right in my face. And I knew I was wounded. It burned pretty bad. And it seemed to hurt too much for just a finger. I had gloves on so I didn't know how bad it was. I couldn't see it. I could see the hole and I knew I'd been hit. And there was blood.

Now, the length of that bank from where I was hidin' to the door was probably twenty, twenty-five feet, so I come and duck walked, stayin' down way below the counter as best as I could to get to the door and get outa there.

At one point between the counter and the door I had to go out into the room of the bank, and I came into his vision again, and I guess he heard me walkin', so he knew I wasn't dead. He still had his weapon and he tried to shoot me in the back, goin' out the door. I saw the bullets hitting the door on either side of me.

Now that was one point where I thought I might shoot this guy. In the process of the robbery I didn't even think about returning fire or defending myself or anything, just gettin' down. I just wanted out of there. But when he tried to shoot me in the back, I thought of returning the fire and shootin' that guy. 'Cause I felt he deserved it. 'Cause I was no longer a threat to him. I was leaving. The robbery was over. He wasn't saying, "Stop." He wasn't sayin' a word. He was just shootin'.

Now, why he missed me I don't know. He didn't miss me by very much. By then I was maybe thirty feet away from him, which wasn't too far. And he came close to hittin' me, close enough so that I was sure he was tryin' to hit me. And it angered me that somebody was tryin' to shoot me in the back after

I was leavin', and I thought about turnin' around and shootin' him. But as soon as I thought that, I knew that if I hit him and did in fact kill him, I'd have to kill them women too, so I kept goin'. I couldn't shoot them. They hadn't done anything wrong to me. I felt that he had done a very severe wrong to me. If they hadn'ta been there, I probably would have shot him. But if they hadn'ta been there, I'd have been robbin' him and he wouldn't have had a chance to pull a gun on me like that. And if somebody else had gone with me, he wouldn't have had a chance to pull a gun. That's another thing.

I grabbed hold of the handle of the door. I hated to do that. I could imagine a bullet going right through my back. But somehow I made it out of there.

Because of the money being stuck in the window, because of the shooting, and because of having to stay low and duck walk out of there, I'd been in there a long time.

I come out and I looked, and the car wasn't there. The getaway car was gone. I figured Joey had heard the shooting and I had been in there a long time, he was circling.

So I turned around and I was headin' back to the bank. I was on the city streets then. I don't even know if I put the gun away. I don't even know if I was on the streets with the gun in my hand or if I had put it in my pocket or what.

I was in complete panic. The car was gone. I figured he'd be looking for me, I don't know what happened. I didn't see him. I don't know what happened to him. With him havin' a record and havin' a lot of suspicion for committing crimes—I suppose he heard the shootin'. He may have assumed, when I didn't come right out, that I was in fact wounded bad and captured or maybe even dead. Perhaps he just took off right after that. He knew that if the police had come, he'd have had a hard time explainin' his presence in an area where a bank had been robbed, especially in a stolen vehicle.

So I was running and running and running. I couldn't find the car. It was gone. And it being the wintertime, I thought that perhaps I'll be able to steal a car. Somebody'll have the motor running to keep the car warm. There wasn't nothin' movin' in that town. There wasn't a bicycle. There wasn't nothin'. And everywhere I looked and I couldn't believe it. I thought, well, if I could get out of the bank, I could get in the car and get away. There wasn't a taxi. There wasn't nothin'. There wasn't a car I could have jumped in and captured if I'd wanted to. There was no traffic. And I ran through the back yards and alleys and streets and things, and it seems like I was out of the bank twenty minutes. Then the police started comin'. I started hearin' sirens and seein' police activity and stuff. The alarm had gone out to off-duty police. The town was suddenly filled with police.

I got down near some shrubbery. A cruiser went by. I got out and started runnin' up through a woodlot. It was snow and ice, and it was hard goin', and my lungs was burning from running so hard and tryin' to get away and the nervous excitement, I suppose. And I felt like I was gonna drop, but I knew I couldn't. I had to keep goin'. My finger hurt bad. My hand hurt bad. I didn't know how bad that was. I thought that maybe the bullet had cut the finger off. I didn't know. There was plenty of blood. It was runnin' out of the hole in the glove. I kept it jammed up tight. I tried to close it into a fist to try to reduce any bleedin'. I didn't know how serious the wound was. I jammed it down in my coat pocket. And I kept runnin'.

14

I crossed a road off a main street. A policeman just happened to be goin' by that intersection at the time I crossed. He saw me. I heard his brakes go on, and he started backin' up real fast. I knew he saw me, and I ran hard as I could. I got up into that ice and snow and stuff. He jumped out of the cruiser and fired some shots at me. I kept runnin', and he's gettin' up over the bank. I don't know how many shots he fired, he kept running, shooting. And I wasn't makin' no progress, so I stopped to surrender.

And he came runnin' up. That was a terrible experience, 'cause he was shakin' like a leaf. The gun was right on my stomach. I think it was a .357 magnum. It was a big gun. It didn't matter what it was. He was scared and agitated, and the gun was on me and was shakin'. He told me not to move and I didn't move. He said, "Where's your gun?"

I said, "It's in my pocket."

He says, "Take it out slow and drop it on the ground. Take it out with your fingertips."

I says, "I'm wounded."

He says, "Drop your gun." He was real gruff.

I says, "All right. I ain't gonna pull nothin'. I surrender." I dropped the gun on the ground.

He was shakin', really shakin', and his finger was tight on the trigger. I thought he was gonna kill me. I really believed it. I asked him to point the gun away. I said, "Man, the thing's gonna go off, the condition you're in." I says, "Look at it. The gun's shakin'." I says, "Just point it off to the side. I ain't gonna do nothin'."

He says, "Just shut up. I'll shoot you right there."

I said, "You're gonna anyway." I said, "If you don't move that gun, it's gonna go off." He wouldn't move it.

Then some other people came, were chargin' up into the woodlot, dressed in civilian clothes. In a little while the bank manager came runnin' up. Four of the people were off-duty police. The manager was insane, angry, fulla hatred. I don't know what possessed him. He was sayin' all kinds of savage remarks. He called me a bastard, a lousy son of a bitch. He said, "I wished I had shot ya." I was standin' there, wounded, with guns on me. There were five or six guns on me then.

They handcuffed me with my hands behind my back. I told 'em I was wounded and asked 'em if they could kinda take it easy. They weren't takin' it easy. In fact, after I got my hands handcuffed behind my back and four of the officers had guns in the back of my head, this arresting officer took a claw—it's a police persuader, it grips you, it's a vice, and they can grab you by the arm or the leg, the collarbone or shoulder, it's a crippling thing, clampin' the flesh right to the bone. And he cranked that thing up on me with my hands handcuffed behind me, and me wounded and four fellow officers with guns on me. With my hands behind my back he put the claw on my left wrist, cranked it down, and he had me right up on my toes and tears comin' out a my eyes.

I said, "What in the hell are you doin'?" I said, "Are you people insane? I gave up. I surrendered. You've got me. What in the hell's with you?"

He said, "Shut up." He was playin' a role, puttin' on a show for the bank manager, I don't know.

One of the other cops says, "Why don't you knock it off?" The other cop had to finally tell him to cut it out 'cause it was gettin' too bad.

Then they took me over to the police station. They took my wallet. I had $322 of my own money with me that I never got back. They gave it to the bank manager. They said it was his money. I said, "It's not so. It was in my wallet." They took it, and I had to pay some bills for the restaurant. The bank manager probably figured I deserved to lose my money. Maybe I did, but he didn't deserve to get it. By law it should have come back to me, but it never did. He kept it.

And I didn't want to give 'em my name 'cause as soon as I stopped to surrender, I thought of my kids and what they were gonna think, that their dad had been caught in a robbery. And that's the first time I thought about anything like that. My mind was on other things besides the police, like what would happen now. I knew I'd go to jail, I worried about California really makin' a move and takin' the kids away. And those things were hittin' me.

The fact I was wounded, I was worried about that, 'cause I'm a musician, and I play with that hand, and I was worried I might be crippled for the rest of my life and not be able to play my music.

They got the bag of money off me that did belong to the bank, and they took my wallet, my money, my address book, my telephone book, which I've never recovered. There's all kinds of valuable contacts and legitimate business—show business—people, bookin' and talent agencies and entertainers, their home phone numbers and office phone numbers, which are very hard for me to replace.

They got me to the police station and they wanted to know

my name. I gave 'em a fake name, which was useless to do 'cause it didn't take them long to go through my wallet and find my driver's license.

They said, "Okay, we're gonna book ya for armed robbery."

I wasn't payin' much attention. All of them other things was goin' through my head—family matters, and the fact that I was wounded.

They didn't keep me in the jail in Merrimack. They took me to Amesbury and put me in jail. And apparently Joey called my home and told my wife that I had been arrested. Anyway, I think it was Joey. I always thought it was. She said, "This is some mistake. Are you kiddin' me?" Or, "This is some kind of joke." She said, "If it's a joke, it's not funny. I don't believe ya." She didn't know that I was engaged in that activity. So she called the Amesbury police station and asked if I was there.

They said, "Yes, he is. Who is callin'?"

She says, "This is his wife. Well, how is he?"

They said, "Well, he's been arrested for armed robbery and he's wounded. At least, he's all right. It's not serious. He's not in any danger from the wound."

I don't know if they told me she was on the phone or what they wanted her to do, or what. But she called a lawyer or Joey had her call him back and he gave her the number of a lawyer. I don't know how all that happened. But she contacted a lawyer and gave him my location, where I was. I don't know what must've entered her mind. It must've been terrible. I don't know when my mother and father found out. She must've called them right away. They've told me all these things since then but I don't know. I know it was just hell for them.

There was a lot of police activity, and the state police came. A representative out of the state prosecutor's office come up and he wanted to talk to me. He was all dressed up and he was bein' real slick. He wanted information. He wanted me to cooperate. He told me that I should, that they could probably help me if I'd help them. He said, "You shouldn't mind talkin', 'cause a lot of big guys are talkin' now, and if they can do it there's no reason why you can't." He says, "Don't be dumb. Don't take the whole rap alone."

125

I says, "Look, I don't want to talk about nothin' right now. I want this hand taken care of. It hurts." I was in agony. It was really hurtin'. 'Cause it wasn't a flesh wound. It hit the bone too.

A state trooper finally took me up to a doctor who had a clinic. The doctor didn't think it was a bullet wound, because my gun had rosewood handles and when the bullet went through my finger and into the handle on the gun, it splintered the handle, and wood splinters had gone into the wound from the back side. The bullet went in, mushroomed, and blew back. That's another reason it might have hurt so much too.

I said, "Well, I don't know. I thought it was a bullet wound." Then, I wasn't sure. My mind wasn't clear then. Well, running, I could've fell against a sharp rock or something. I was confused. I thought I remembered lookin', after the gunshot, and seein' the hole in the glove and blood and stuff. Then I couldn't remember, maybe I did fall and hit somethin' and in the excitement and panic and everythin' I didn't feel it. It didn't make sense to me. Then the X rays showed the shattering of the bone and all that. It was a bullet wound. He treated it and said he was worried about infection. He said I should have a lot of care on that. And I guess he gave me antibiotics and pain pills.

They took me back to the Amesbury jail. And this detective, or whatever he was, from the state prosecutor's office come down and he wanted to talk some more. And I told him I wasn't gonna talk. I wanted my lawyer and he could talk to the lawyer and the lawyer would tell him everything he wanted to know, after I saw the lawyer.

I stayed in that jail. The police in Amesbury were pretty nice guys. I had got a bad opinion of police. I had developed it even though a lot of my friends were law enforcement people, out west and down south. But these guys at the Amesbury station were really good guys. They were concerned that I was in pain and havin' difficulty and in real serious trouble with the law. These men told me that my wife had called. They told me that the lawyer had called up and told me not to say anything and for me to take it easy and they'd see me in the morning. I was gonna be arraigned upstairs in the mornin'. They have a court right over the jail in Amesbury. They take you up the back stairs, all chained together.

I was feelin' pretty bad and I spent a rough night with a wounded hand, and they brought in some drunk and put him in the cell behind me, and he kept kickin' the wall all night long. I screamed at him. I told him if he kept it up, I was goin' to try to get the police to open the doors and I'd come over there and smack him 'cause he was just bein' obnoxious and screamin' and hollerin' and threatenin'.

He told me he was gonna cut my head off. He was antagonizin' me.

I says, "You punk." I says, "Hey, I don't need any gaff from you. You creep." I says, "I just got shot in a friggin' bank and I'm not gonna listen to your shit."

He says, "Oh, I'm sorry. I'm sorry. I thought you was a drunk. I thought you was a wise guy." You see, he had found out. I guess he heard it on the news or somethin' that there had been a robbery. He cooled it when he found out that I was a suspect. He calmed right down. But he kept me awake most of the night, plus the pain from the hand.

Funny thing. The police got a crank call in Amesbury, while I was in their jail. Now, it was on the TV and radio and everything—my name and where I was from, there'd been a shooting and, you know, attempted bank robbery. It was on all the news. Some nut called up the police station and said they were comin' down to bust me out. Now, that wasn't Joey or Vince or any of my friends or anybody I knew. They wouldn't do somethin' stupid like that.

They had a bright light on. They went out back and chained the door closed, the back door to the police station was chained and locked with a padlock from the inside. And I asked the cop why the light was left on. I said, "The light's awful bright." And he sat right there watchin' me, right in front of my cell. All night long, the cop was there. And I said, "How come the light? And why are you sittin' here like this?"

He says, "Well, we got a call that they're gonna come and bust you out, and we ain't takin' no chances."

So the cops stayed on me twenty-four hours. And I think that call hurt me real bad, the way I was handled by the police after that and after I was arraigned. They took it serious. They probably realized it was a crank, but they weren't takin' no chances, like the cop said.

After arraignment, I saw the lawyer. He said, "Don't say nothin'. Don't talk to nobody. Tell 'em that you have a lawyer and to see your lawyer. If they want to talk to you, I want to be present. Don't say nothin' if I'm not present. It's vital to your defense." He instructed me in all them things. He said he'd be in touch with me. He told me I'd probably be taken to one of the county jails, rather than keep me there. He said they did in fact receive a threat the night before and they were uptight about me. They didn't know who I was and they were checkin' me out, and I'd probably have it a little bit rough for a while on account of that.

I did in fact have it rough. They took me to Lawrence Jail and put me in maximum security and kept everybody away from me. I couldn't even move. I couldn't get phone calls. I couldn't do anything.

I think it was that afternoon that my dad, mother, wife came down to see me. I wanted to see the kids but I didn't wanta see them right then. They were concerned about my health and my hand and gettin' me out of that jail. They didn't ask me how I got there. No, they didn't go into that then. They have since. I think to this day my mother believes I was forced into it. She thinks that I was intimidated and coerced and all that stuff. You know how mothers are.

I talked about bail, and bail had been set at $20,000. And my lawyer talked to the judge, at the time of the arraignment when they set bail, about no record. He wanted it cut down to $5,000. The judge wouldn't, but cut it to $15,000.

I stayed in Lawrence Jail for three days. My father put up 10 percent, to get a bondsman to come down. That was more than a thousand dollars. Things moved slow. The bondsman came down on the third day. It was nighttime. And I think I got out at ten or ten-thirty at night.

So after three days I bailed out of Lawrence. I couldn't stand that jail. There was no toilets, no runnin' water. It looked like a horror movie that Alfred Hitchcock put together. I didn't believe things like that existed. All these experiences were new to me. I think that if you're gonna lock a man up like an animal he should have a toilet and he should have water available to him. It was a terrible, terrible experience, that jail, and the whole thing was a terrible experience before the jail. But on the third night my dad and my wife came down with the bondsman, and I returned to my home in Portsmouth.

15

They had taken my personal money when I was arrested for the robbery in Merrimack, and I didn't have any money and the family didn't have any, and supplies and things were gettin' low in the house. So I went to work, which was difficult 'cause I was playin' the steel guitar and my hand was wounded. I took the heavy bandage off and wrapped my finger lightly so I could play. It was painful, but I did it.

We played one night, and it was a one-night stand. The drummer didn't have an automobile. I took him home, it was maybe one-thirty or two in the morning. We was unloading his drums and things at his place out on the sidewalk and it was pretty still and quiet at that time of the day. There was an all-black car driving around. Something was strange about it, the way it was driving around and stuff. I got paranoid. I didn't know who it was. It was one person in the car, and I couldn't see who it was. And this black car was roaming around this block where we were unloading these drums. I didn't know if somebody might try to take revenge on me for the crimes.

The car pulled up several car spaces behind me, and the person inside got out of the car and started to walk toward me. I spun around. I told him to hold it. I said, "Don't bother comin' any closer. State your business.

And he says, "I'm a police officer."

I says "You got some identification?"

He says, "Yeah."

I says, "All right. Show it." He did identify himself. He says, "You're Warren Hart, I thought you was in jail."

I says, "You know better than that. You people aren't so distant that you don't know I've been bailed out. You know that I was in and I made bail and now I'm out and in the community. I'm back home." I said, "Let's not try to jive each other." I don't know how long he had been following me but I had been watching him for a few minutes. I said, "You're kind of stupid." And I told him he had made me nervous. I said, "Your car doesn't indicate that it's a police car. I don't know you. You're comin' up at me at two in the mornin' after the situation that I've been through." I said, "You're not dressed in some kind of a uniform. You're dressed in some kind of a suit, and I don't know if you mean me any harm or not." I said, "Somebody might shoot you someday for that."

He said, "I didn't think of that." And he said, "I just wanted to check. I thought you was in jail." And he drove off. I don't know where he picked up on me.

16

I was out on bail three days. I played, a couple of the nights. My friends, the people I worked with, knew I had been shot, knew I had been arrested, and knew I was out on bail. They didn't ask about it. They're not that kind of people. They just told me that if there's any way they could help to let 'em know. And they probably thought it wasn't too serious if I had just been arrested and was right out. That seemed to be the attitude, that it couldn't be too serious.

Anyway, I was out three days, and I went shopping with my wife and little daughter. And this was in the wintertime, so it got dark early. And I went up to J. M. Fields in the shopping center and bought groceries from the money I had earned playing. I was supposed to play that night. In fact, in a couple of nights we planned to open in the Holiday Inn with a big engagement and a lot of publicity. That was a big break for the band.

I came home from buying the groceries. My daughter was only two years old. She was just a baby, and my wife was carryin' her in her arms. I was carryin' two bags of groceries, and we stepped out of the car.

Across the street from our house was a parkin' lot. It was all dark. There was some cars over there. You couldn't see. And I had two big bags of groceries in my arms. My wife is standin' beside me with the baby in her arms.

A voice called out in the dark, "Warren Hart, don't move. You're under arrest. If you move, we'll shoot." And somebody started walkin' towards me.

I could see the gun first and I was greatly concerned about my daughter and her mother. I told 'em "I'm not movin'." I couldn't move if I wanted to.

They come up to me and said, "Don't make any quick moves. Put the groceries on the car."

I told my wife to take the baby inside. I says, "She's goin' in, all right?"

He says, "Yeah, don't you move till we tell you to."

I said to her, "Just go in the house. It'll be all right." She was shocked and frightened. She had never seen nothing like that.

I put the groceries up on the hood of the car. Then they searched me down. They told me they were there to arrest me for armed robbery.

I got angry. I says, "Somebody's playin' games. I don't know what in the hell you guys are doin'. I just been arrested for robbery. In fact, I just got out on bail on $15,000. Somebody better get their stuff together." I said, "Who the hell sent you up here, anyway?"

He said, "Man, I don't know nothin' about it. All I got is an order that you're to be arrested. If we see you, we are to take you into custody.

I says, "Well, look, this is ridiculous. I'm out on bail. Somebody's gonna be sued for it or somethin'. I'm not gonna fool around with this crap. I got a family. You scared the hell out of my wife and my daughter who was there. You got your guns

131

drawn, endangerin' them. I'm not armed, and I'm out on bail. You should know that. What's the matter with your police station? This is the second time that somebody's bugged me from your department."

He said, "I don't know." He was a pretty nice guy. He knew me before, from playin', the restaurant, and on the street. I dove with some of the guys, scuba diving. He said, "I don't know nothin' about it."

I said, "Well, look, can we go inside?" It was wintertime. I said, "It's cold. I got to bring the groceries in. I got no gun. I'm out on bail. I'm clean." I said, "You call your department and find out if there is any chance of some mistake. And I definitely want to call my lawyer, and I'd just as soon call from home as from down at the police station, if that's where we're goin'."

He said, "I don't see nothin' wrong with that," and he asked his partner if he saw anything wrong with that. He said, "No." They were pretty decent. We went in the house, and the dogs were excited. I had a German shepherd, a big one, and a cock-a-poodle, and they were both excited. I calmed them down.

My wife was in pretty bad shape. I told her, "It's a mistake. There must be some mistake. We made the bail. You come down with Dad and made the bail." I said, "They'll get it straightened out."

She said, "I hope so. I can't take much more of this."

So they called up, and they said there was definitely a warrant for my pickup. The New Hampshire state police had a warrant for them to pick me up for bank robbery. So I called my lawyer and he said, "What in the hell is goin' on?"

I said, "The police are here, and they've just told me that they've got a warrant for my arrest for a robbery at a bank, and they want to take me in."

He says, "Well, go with 'em. Don't give 'em any trouble, if they got a signed warrant. I'll check to make sure it's legal. Don't give 'em any hassle." He says, "I'll be up to see you as soon as I can."

So they took me into custody. They took me down to the police station, and I asked 'em about the robbery. And they said,

"Well, it wasn't a Massachusetts robbery, it was a bank in New Hampshire. It was another one."

I said, "Great."

17

I was in the cell in the Portsmouth city jail, and I told my wife to call my father, let him know what had happened, and if she needed anything to make sure and let him know. I knew I was gonna be in a hassle then, but I did expect the lawyers and my friends to come through and get me out in a week. But I knew my wife and the kids would need grocery money and things like that, so I told her, "Don't worry. We'll get it straightened out. It's obviously a mistake. If you need anything before it's straightened out, call up the folks or stay with them or have them bring you whatever you need." You see, all the money that I had was spent on the groceries.

They got me down to the police station. They put me in a stupid cell with hardwood boards. That's all there was for a bunk in it. I was only there for three-quarters of an hour, and some detective wanted to talk to me upstairs. He had this big book. He opened it up and it was as big as a kitchen table, I guess, a big ledger book. The pages had red marks in 'em and blue ink and stuff. And he wanted me to confess to a whole bunch of crimes that had been committed in the area.

I said, "Man, you're crazy."

He says, "Well, these are crimes that have been committed in the last few months and they aren't solved yet and we're pretty sure you done it. And, uh, they're not all that serious, these crimes. Why don't you get if off your chest and confess?" He said, "You're facin' a pretty serious charge, armed robbery. Just get it all gathered up together in one package for the judge and it probably won't make much difference. And we can clean our books up. And you can have a clear conscience."

I said, "I don't even know what you're talkin' about. And if you think I'm gonna plead guilty to somethin' I didn't do, then you're insane." I said, "I wouldn't even plead guilty if I done it, to you." I said, "That's your job, to prove it. If you think I done it, prove it." I said, "But some of those things you're accusin' me of, if you check it out you'll find out that I couldn't possibly be there. Nobody can be in two places at the same time." I says, "One of the things you're tryin' to accuse me of, I was in the Lawrence jail when it happened. How in the hell do you explain that, if you got such good information?"

He said, "Well, I can be wrong about that."

I said, "You're wrong about the whole thing."

He said, "What's so-an-so got against you?" He named a guy's name, an informer, a rat, somebody in the community that hung around. He was a kind of a bum and a sneak-thief and things like that. I knew him. I knew him in the community, and I knew he was no good, and I didn't associate with him. He knew some people that I knew and he might sit in a booth with us, but not from my invitation, and he'd have a cup of coffee or somethin'. He was a creep. He said, "What's this guy got against you?"

I said, "What do you mean, what's he got against me? He's got nothin' against me."

He said, "Well he told us you done all this." He says, "Forget I said that."

I says, "Yeah, I'll forget it." I says, "I don't know. Maybe I went out with one of his girl friends. How do I know? What better way to hurt a guy than with this kind of crap?" I says, "Why didn't you talk to me about this before?"

He says, "Well, that's the only thing we had. It wasn't very strong. We didn't have any evidence."

I says, "Well, you ain't got nothin' now. You got even less." I says, "You better check out your supply of information. You don't have very good informers." I said, "I don't want to talk any more about this crap. If you're gonna charge me with it, then charge me with it. And I want my lawyer. I ain't going to play no more games with you."

He says, "Well, you're going back downstairs anyway." He says, "Forget it." And that was the last I heard about that.

I was in the cell about a half hour after that incident, and I don't know if they were settin' this up or what, just harassin' me or playin' mind games or what. But in come some police in a uniform that was strange to me. I'd never seen the uniform before—different colors, like green and brown, and I was used to blue. They come by my cell and they're lookin' me all over. They're turnin' their heads and lookin' at me like I'm some specimen on display. And I started swearin' at 'em. "Get the hell out of here. What do you guys want? Don't bug me." I didn't feel good. I was angry, and upset. I was nervous. My finger still hurt pretty bad.

They said, "Well, he fits the description."

I said, "Fuck you." I'm sayin' to myself "Here we go again." But it wasn't funny.

They said, "Where were you between five-thirty and six tonight?"

I says, "Look, I don't have to talk to you at all. I don't know what kind of game you're playing. But I don't have nothin' to worry about, 'cause I was arrested tonight shortly after that time."

They said, "We know that. That's why we're talkin' to you. Where were you between five-thirty and six?" I was arrested about six.

I says, "You know damn well where I was. I was grocery shoppin'."

They said, "Yeah, you were shoppin' all right, but it wasn't for groceries. You were robbin' some store down in Rye." Some grocery store got robbed, right at that time when I went to get groceries with my wife and daughter. And they said I fit the description.

I said, "Well, why don't you blame me for every friggin' crime that's happened in the whole state from the time I was born? You can't blame me for stuff before that, can you?" I says, "You're insane. I was up to the store. The cashier can identify me, probably. If she can't, that's not too surprising, 'cause

135

there's a million people there. I don't know the people up there personally, all of them. But I'll tell you, I was there. I went grocery shoppin'. The groceries are at home. The slip is probably still in the bag." I said, "Just keep away from my family, that's all. 'Cause I'm sick of you."

They said, "Well, you're goin' into a lineup."

I says, "I am, like hell."

They says, "Well, what have you got to hide?"

I says, "I ain't got nothin' to hide, but I ain't goin' into one of your phony lineups."

They says, "You are too."

I says, "Well, my lawyer's not here. Before I go into any lineup, I want to talk to him." And he had already told me to do that.

They said, "Get out of the cell. Come out here."

I went with 'em. And it was the stupidest thing you've ever seen. They had this lineup on the second floor. They didn't even have a lineup room or an ID room where the lights was on you and stuff. It was out like in the hallway, in a corridor or somethin', at the head of the stairs. And this lady that had been robbed was in another room, off the corridor.

They had me and some other people lined up. They had cops in trench coats and all kinds of stuff and I guess people they grabbed off the street. I don't know who they were. They had six or seven people it seemed like, standin' up against the wall, and they told me to go over there and stand against the wall.

I says, "I'm not gonna stand there. I want my lawyer."

One of the policemen pointed at some strangers observing. He says, "There's your lawyer."

I said, "You're out of your mind. I don't even know that guy. That's *your* lawyer. He's gotta be your lawyer or he wouldn't be here. He's not here for me."

They brought the woman out into the corridor, and they said, "Well, stand over there anyway. He is your lawyer."

I says, "He ain't my lawyer. I'm not concedin' to that. I'm not allowing that. If you pursue this and it goes to court, I'm goin' to tell 'em exactly what's happened here." I said, "You guys are crazy. It's illegal as hell, I know that much."

They said, "Well, we're not gonna argue with you. Get over there. 'Cause we can make you get over there."

I says, "Okay. Under threat, I'll go over there. But I'm not goin' over there 'cause you're tellin' me he's my lawyer." So I went over there under threat, under protest.

They brought this woman out, and she was excited. And she come up and down the line. She was supposed to look us all over and see if the one that robbed her was there and point him out.

Well, she looked us all over and she says, "No. He's not there."

I started to laugh, and they got mad. They said, "Isn't that him?" And they kept pointin' right at me. She come back and looked. She got right in front of my face, four inches away, and looked me all over.

I was shakin' my head. I says, "You guys are somethin'."

He says, "Shut up." And they said, "Repeat after me: 'This is a holdup. Give me all the money'."

I says, "I will, like hell." I says, "You're crazy. Anyone sayin' them words is gonna sound like he's guilty of somethin'. And I'm not gonna say it."

They says, "She just wants to hear your voice."

I said, "She can hear my voice now."

"Yeh, but you gotta say them words."

I said, "Yeah. You say them if you ever get grabbed."

So they took her back into the room, and I could hear 'em in there. She wouldn't identify me, and they were browbeatin' her. I could hear their voices. They said, "We're sure that's him. Can't you make an identification? That's all we need."

She said, "No, I can't be sure that's him." She says, "I'm not sure of anything right now. I'm awfully nervous." She says, "It may be him, but I can't say that it is with absolute certainty."

They were mad at her, and they were mad at me, and they yanked me off the corridor and dragged me back to the cell.

I says, "Are you guys done? Have you had your fun for the night? How about just leavin' me the hell alone?"

They said, "You think you're wise, don't you? You think you're smart?" They said, "We're goin' up to your house."

I said, "Well, don't take it out on the family 'cause you didn't get somebody to identify me for a crime I didn't do. Leave them the hell alone."

They said, "We're goin' up there anyway. We got a warrant and we're gonna look for that bank money you stole."

I says, "Don't bug me. You just better stay within the law yourself or you'll be in court, that's all." I says, "I ain't takin' no more of your crap."

A couple of guys down there, they come in on duty and they calmed it down. They said, "Leave him the hell alone. We've known him a long time. He ain't a bad guy. He never give us trouble." They got on them for hasslin' me, a couple of friends of mine that knew me, so that eased the situation a little bit.

Well, they went to the house. They went out with a warrant. They asked me for the keys to my car, and I said, "I ain't got none." I says, "I don't have nothin'. Anything I had on me, you guys took it." I had two cars. I had to park my Cadillac for the winter in my garage because there was water in the gasoline and some sand and stuff. It was givin' me trouble in the cold months, so I put it up and was gonna work on it in the spring. I had already transferred the plates. The plates were off it. They said, "You got two cars. Where's the keys to the car you got parked?"

I said, "They're at home, as far as I know. My wife will give 'em to you."

They went up to the house, and they were gone for maybe a half, three-quarters of an hour, and they come back. I didn't live far from town, only a few minutes away. And one of the cops says, "What in the hell have you got in that house?"

I said, "What do you mean?"

He said, "Well, when we knocked on the door, it sounded like some five-hundred-pound gorilla in there or something, screamin' and tryin' to get at us and everythin'." They said, "We wouldn't go in. We asked for the keys to the car and your wife started to open the door but we wouldn't let her open it. We had her pass the keys through the mail slot in the door." They said, "What have you got in that house?"

I said, "It's only a German shepherd. He'll sit in your lap."

138

He says, "Like hell. I wouldn't go in that house for a million dollars. I'd quit my job first." What it was, was the cock-a-poodle. It was worse than the German shepherd. Both of 'em were barkin' and carryin' on. They probably sensed that my wife was nervous and maybe they knew that earlier the police took me away. I don't know how intelligent animals are, but they aren't stupid. They were barkin', and she couldn't quiet 'em down. The police wouldn't go in that house, and the house was never searched with that warrant. With an armed robbery, everything could have been sittin' in there in the living room coffee table and it would've been safe because they wouldn't go in.

They got the keys and they went over to my car, the Cadillac. Now, some friends of mine had broke into a doctor's place or a dentist's office, somethin' to do with medical. And they didn't want to keep the stuff at their house, and they asked me, "Could we stash it somewhere? How about your car? Can we just leave this in your car for a few days until we can unload it?"

I said, "Look. I don't know nothin' about it. If you want to take the keys, if you want to fool around with my car, that's up to you. It's on you." I said, "If you're smart, you won't leave fingerprints and all that kind of stuff." I was in the robberies. I wasn't in that petty crap. They asked me a favor, and they were some friends of mine, people I considered friends. And if they asked a favor, I did it, because they would for me. They weren't low people, in my mind. So it was theirs, it wasn't mine. And they had a plastic wastebasket, much bigger than five gallons. I don't know how big it was. Like a small trash can. It was large. And they had put it in the trunk of the car, and it was filled with all kinds of drug paraphernalia. Well, I guess the police about went out of their minds when they saw it, when they searched my car in connection with the robbery. I told them my car was off the road. But that didn't make no difference. They searched it anyway.

And they come back and I knew they'd been in the car. I don't know why they didn't get a warrant and go right back down there and impound that stuff, but they didn't. They waited. And I can't remember if it was on the phone or in person, I told my wife, I says, "Look. Call this number and tell the people what's happened to me, that I've been arrested, in case they haven't read about it in the papers." I says, "Also tell 'em that the car has been searched and that they'd better get things taken care of."

She says, "What do you mean?"

I says, "That's enough. That's all you're gonna know. That's all you need to know." I says, "Just deliver that message. They've still got time, so far as I know, to take care of things."

She says, "All right, I'll give the message." She didn't know what to do. She done what I told her. And that was the only message she delivered, but it was enough, 'cause the police did in fact go out there with a warrant against me for the possession of a bunch of drug paraphernalia. And I would've got hit with that.

They went back out there and the car was empty, and they were hostile. They were really mad. They come back down to me in the jail. They were concerned. They said, "We don't know how you done it but we know what was in that car."

I said, "I don't know what you're talkin' about. I don't know what was in that car. The car's been parked there for months. What're you talkin' about?

They said, "You're pretty clever, ain't you?"

I said, "I don't know what you're talkin' about. You're gonna have to be more clear if we're gonna talk."

They said, "The night we went over there and we couldn't get into the house because of the dogs and stuff, we went and did search the car. And when we opened the trunk, we couldn't believe our eyes. And you know what was in there. It was your stuff."

I said, "I don't know what was in there."

He says, "I'll tell you what was in there. There was drugs and hypodermic needles. There was all kinds of stuff. You wouldn't believe what was in there. There was a basket full of it. And we want it."

I said, "I don't know what you're talkin' about." And I didn't know what was in there. I didn't know what they put in there. I didn't know what they'd stolen. I didn't care. As far as I was concerned, they asked if they could put somethin' in there and I said okay and that was the extent of all I wanted to know about it. And I didn't know what was in there.

They said, "Look, you're gonna get in serious trouble. This is worse than the other thing, and we're gonna come down on you hard. This is narcotics." You know how they were on narcotics in '70.

I says, "Man, I didn't put that in there. I don't know what you're talkin' about. If you say it was there, why the hell didn't you take it then?"

They said, "You know we can't without a warrant. And when we did get the warrant and go back, the car is empty, the car is clean. Now, somebody removed that. You had somebody remove that out of there."

I said, "I've been in jail, you fool. In fact, I lost my keys to that car. I didn't have those keys, and the only set are home, the ones that are on my wife's ring. She has an extra set of keys for the Cadillac." I said, "I don't even have the house key. I got the keys to the Ford. My house key and the Cadillac key, I lost 'em. The only set of keys is the one she gave you so that you could get in the car." Well, my friends had the keys. That's how they got into the car.

Well, they didn't like it. They said, "Look. You're clever. You're smart. We went out there to pull a bust on you for the narcotics. We'd rather get you on that than on the armed robbery. But we'll make a deal with ya. If you'll get those things and give them to us, nothin' will be said about it."

I said, "You must think I'm very, very stupid—and you tell me I'm sharp—if I did have a bunch of drugs, get 'em away from you somehow while I'm in jail, locked up, and then turn around and give 'em back to you on just your word that you're not gonna do anything about it."

They said, "Look, it's important to us. It's more important than catching you to see those things destroyed."

I says, "Well, I don't know what I can tell you. I don't have 'em. I don't know where they are, and I can't give 'em to you." They were very mad about that.

18

I spent four months in the Brentwood County Farm awaitin' trial for the Epping job. I couldn't make bail. The bank I robbed so happens to be owned by a board of directors, and who's on the board of directors but the judge that set my bail and the chief of police of the town that the bank was robbed in. First the bail was set at $10,000. I was already out on $15,000, but they wouldn't give me personal recognizance knowing that that bondsman in Massachusetts would come after me just as strong as if I got a bondsman in New Hampshire. They didn't give me a break at all. I didn't see my lawyer. He was a Massachusetts lawyer, and he had to associate with a lawyer in New Hampshire so that he could appear in courts in New Hampshire. And I wish I had never got him, 'cause he's a fireball lawyer. He's a good lawyer but he angered the court. The court was already angry with him before I got him.

I was up against it from the word go. Six months earlier I went before that same courtroom, with the same judge, the same prosecutor, as an alibi witness for Tom Walker, who was workin' in my restaurant. Now, that judge should have disqualified himself, and that's grounds for reversal right there. That judge was prejudiced, and he showed it in many ways. The very fact that he sat on a case before, where I was an alibi witness for a man that was convicted, should automatically disqualify him. I didn't know these things until I came to prison. I didn't know nothin' about it. My lawyer should've but he wasn't the lawyer that had been involved in Tom's trial and he didn't know that.

Another thing going against me, that very same lawyer within that year had successfully defended three people from out of state on a first-degree murder charge and beat the state. They won the case and walked out of there free people, and he was the lawyer. Same court, same people involved, same bailiff. And they all knew him and they hated him. He made 'em look foolish and they hated his guts. I didn't know that. So I had it stacked against me pretty much the whole way.

And you show me one jury, in this state or any state, that happens to be a jury of your peers. That is a joke. They're professional jurors. They hang around the courtroom. They loll around the corridors, waitin' for assignment to jury duty. They ain't hard-workin' men. Hard-workin' men don't hang around the courtroom like vultures, panderin' to the judges, nodding and bowing. No, the ones who sit on juries are friends of the court. They're friends of the judge.

You know how I was identified? From the photograph of me, the mug shot, taken after arrest in Amesbury. Wounded, just been caught in that condition I described when the car was gone, I was frantic, wild, scared to death. And they had a photograph of me. And they put my photograph in with twelve others. And they took it to the teller at the bank in Epping, to her home, at night. My photograph amongst twelve others. Now, in those thirteen photographs, I was the only one that had blond hair and sharp features. I was the only one that in any way resembled the person that was the bank robber. And on the back of the picture, typed in red of all things, my name, physical description, the date of arrest, and that I was a suspect for bank robbery. This is all in the back of the photograph. The person reads it and then identifies me. Then they let the jury see it, and they find me guilty. It's all illegal. That photograph done irreparable harm to me, and the way it was presented to the person. There should have been several people in there with my complexion, coloring, and build. No, they were short, fat, dark, black-haired, Italians. I was the only one. It was illegal.

And there's other events during the trial that I want to talk about too, like bein' shoved around in handcuffs in front of the jury by the sheriffs. Like lettin' the door of the elevator slam in the face of one of the jurors when she was tryin' to enter the elevator with us. It was very rude. I was in handcuffs. I couldn't hold the door for her.

You should see what goes on behind closed doors and in the corridors and in back rooms. I can tell you more about that trial, how the witnesses were coached. It's a stage play. Whoever writes the best script wins.

Another thing that made it bad and made it impossible for justice is that I did have these things hangin' over me in Massachusetts.

My lawyer had me take the stand. Now, how the hell are you gonna conduct yourself under cross-examination and not say somethin' that's gonna incriminate you on pending charges in a sister state, with their representatives possibly sittin' in the courtroom and who are gonna take it down as evidence, and not be evasive and not look bad to the judge and to the jury? The prosecutor knew that. He knew I was out on bail for charges in Massachusetts. He didn't bring it up. He was too smart for that. But he knew I couldn't answer questions. He knew I couldn't talk about guns too well without gettin' tripped up, 'cause I did own guns. I've owned guns all my life, and I did use a gun in robberies. I couldn't say much. I couldn't really defend myself, and I had to spend too much time thinkin' about what I said that wouldn't get me in trouble in Massachusetts, so that I looked real bad in New Hampshire. I'd had it. But there was no choice. If I didn't take the stand, what was the jury gonna think? And how can you stand up and tell the jury, "Well, this man is wanted in Massachusetts for crimes, and he can't speak without jeopardizing himself down there." They had me.

I pleaded not guilty 'cause the lawyer advised it and because I was scared and because I had never been through an experience like that before, personally, in my life. Today, if I'd done something wrong, I'd stand up and I'd say so and I'd take my punishment. It would have been the smart thing to do as well as the right thing to do.

I got ten to twenty years at the New Hampshire state prison in Concord. That's what the judge gave me for a sentence after the jury decided I was guilty. If you'd check it out you'd probably see that, for that type of crime, I'm the most heavily punished of anybody in the history of the state.

You can't imagine what it was like in the courtroom when the judge announced the sentence. It was terrible. I couldn't say nothin'. I sank back. It was a death sentence. My family was there, and they started cryin'. It almost killed my father. It was a terrible experience. I would never put nobody through that again. If I wanted to rob the Chase Manhattan Bank in New York City and had a 99.9 percent chance of gettin' away with it, with all their millions of dollars, I wouldn't do it if there was that one chance in a thousand of me bein' caught. Or I'd shoot some-body, and I don't want that. I know me. I escalate fast, because I don't believe in diggin' ditches by hand all your life when you got a tractor there.

Donna came over to visit me at the jail the next day, and I told her, I says, "Look," I says, "I don't believe what the lawyers say about the appeals and that I'll be out and all that. I've had it. That's way too much time." I says, "Why don't you just forget me?" I says, "It'll probably hurt you for a while. But you'll get over it."

But here I am talkin' to a girl that I've been with for four or five years, as husband and wife, day and night, raisin' a family to-gether, and I'm tellin' her to get out. And she just ain't listenin' to it. She just didn't want to hear no more of it. She says to me, "That's the same thing as you sayin' you don't trust me."

I says, "No, it ain't at all. I'm just bein' realistic." I says, "Ten to twenty years is an awful long time, and I still got Massachu-setts to face. We don't know what's gonna happen down there."

She says, "I don't care." She says, "I don't want you to tell me to leave no more. I'm not gonna leave ya. I'm gonna stick by ya."

So I said, "Okay. It's up to you. I'm not askin' you to. I wouldn't ask nobody to do anythin' like that. That's too much."

19

You read about prison life and you see it on the movies and TV. It's called the slammer and there's always that steel door slam-min' behind ya and the first time you hear it, it's shockin'. And you know you're not goin' out for a long, long time. And you look ahead and everythin's unknown. You don't know what's going to happen. You've heard stories about prisons and the violence and all kinds of things. A lot of it's fantasy and unreal. You're a street person still, in your mind. In reality, you're a prisoner.

My lawyer was supposed to see me. I was sentenced on a Wednesday. He says, "Well, you'll be goin' up to the joint. And I'll see ya on Friday." And I never seen him since, to this day. That was wearin' away on my nerves, too, because I figured there would be an appeal, at least on the sentencing aspect because it was very, very severe. It was almost inhuman. But I didn't see the lawyer, and I kept tryin' to contact him, and he wouldn't answer my letters even.

Visits were only one hour every two weeks then, and a good part of the visits were spent on a desperate attempt to find out if my family was aware of the importance of gettin' in touch with the lawyer and appealin' the sentence. He wouldn't answer their phone calls. He wouldn't talk to them on the phone. He wouldn't respond to nobody. If I'd known then what I know now, I'd have put in a complaint through the grievance procedure of the American Bar Association or the state bar association, get him censured, get somebody with authority to say, "Hey, what the hell you doin' with this guy?" But I didn't know those things. I was kind of a babe in the woods in a lot of areas. For a long time I had hopes of gettin' the sentence reduced, but after three years I gave up on it. I became very bitter, fast. At the prison. At the law. At the whole system. At the invisible thing that surrounded me. In addition to the wall around the prison, there was something around me and it was pressing in on me. I wanted to kill the thing. I really wanted to kill the injustice, the unfairness, the hurt that was being perpetrated on my family by my actions. Things that you couldn't put your finger on I wanted to kill. I didn't want to kill people, although at one time I probably would've shot that foolish lawyer if I could've seen him, at least in the leg I would've shot him, because he lied to me and he hurt me and he hurt my family.

I was goin' insane. For eight months I was goin' through pure hell. Like they had a Christmas tree down in the dinin' hall, and I wanted to tear that thing to shreds. I thought that was the most awful joke that anyone ever perpetrated on a group of people, to put up a Christmas tree in the middle of a goddamn maximum security prison when you're gonna be away from your family. I still think it's hideous.

146

Donna helped me in a lot of ways. I was bitter and she would counsel me. She'd say, "Well, you're not gonna help yourself by feelin' that way. You're gonna have to just be strong and be patient. Everything will work out in the end." She says, "I do promise you that. No matter what happens. In the end, everything will work out."

Oh, sometimes, maybe, when she was in a bad mood or things were goin' rough or maybe finances were rough for her or she was extra lonesome or somethin', she might say in passing, "Why did you ever have to do that? We shouldn't have to live like this. The kids need ya. I need ya." But she didn't punish me. I knew she was hurtin'. She just would talk like that when she was in a real bad mood, and then I'd pick her up. It was pretty nice, too, because if I was in a particularly good mood, then she could let herself go and I'd strengthen her. If I was in a bad mood, she'd be the one who was strong and strengthen me. It worked out pretty good.

We'd meet in our thoughts, maybe at eleven o'clock the night of a visit. We'd set this up. And pretty soon it was almost like you'd be right together. I am not one to say that there isn't such a thing as astral projection, because sometimes you'd feel a person's presence and influence just as much as if they were sitting right beside you. She'd write and say, "Gee, I had the strongest feeling about you last night at suppertime. What were you doing?" And I had her picture down at that time and I was looking at it. And there was a strong concentration on my part, focused on her, and she felt it.

She had to work. She didn't have much success with the welfare. She didn't get welfare. She went for some assistance of food at one of the offices in the town, and some worker there gave her a bad time and insulted her. She felt insulted and demeaned by it and less of a person. She told me, "I'm not goin' back." She said, "I don't care if I have to work my fingers to the bone. I'm not gonna put up with those insults, makes you feel like a dog beggin' for a bone."

I said, "Well, look, those kids are my kids, and they got a right to be taken care of." I says, "It's up to you."

She says, "I'll take care of 'em. But I'm not gonna go through any more of that kind of thing and be insulted by people like that." And she didn't. I was real proud of her. She did go to work, and she was only gettin' $1.65 an hour, workin' in a nursing home. There ain't nothin' about that girl that I ain't proud of her for.

I began to think more seriously about my religion than I had ever done before. I told Donna I realized that if I had honored my priesthood and had been living my life the way I should, none of this would have happened. I told her I was sorry because I knew very well that's what I should've been doin'. I more or less apologized to her for causin' the trouble that I did cause by not practicing the religion.

I've never lied to Donna. One of the hardest things I've ever done is when she come up one time and we was visitin' and she asked me if I ever cheated on her during the time we was together. I had. Not that much, but I had. When I was committing the crimes, that's when I was kinda wild. Well, when I felt like my sexual needs had to be fulfilled, she might have to be preparin' the boys' lunch comin' home from school. There was all kinds of interference that way because of my erratic hours. Sometimes I'd be insistent and after a while I felt like it was rejection, which it wasn't, 'cause she loved me, she almost worshipped me. It was just an impossible situation, so I started to look elsewhere for that fulfillment and I found it. But I still loved her. You see, a man can do that much easier than a woman can. I think a man can go out, once he starts along those lines, can go out and sleep around all over the country and still go home and he wouldn't meet a woman that could make him divorce his wife and leave home. But it's not that easy for a woman. They have to attach love and some kind of emotional entanglement in it, where for a man it's just the sex act and the sex act alone. As far as a man callin' it love, he's much more reluctant to call it love than a woman is.

20

The first job I had in the prison was in the print shop. They had a print shop there where the inmates printed booklets and things for state agencies, and I was one of the inmates workin' there. And there was a series of little fires in the building, nuisance things, nothing serious. They were either detected and put out before they became troublesome or they were so small that they went out by themselves. Somebody just wanted to harass or they didn't know how to set the building on fire. It was just a bunch of little things, aggravatin'. And after a dozen or fifteen of those things, they took ten of us out of the print shop automatically because, with our attitudes and things, ten of us were suspects. But not accusin' us of anything, just yankin' us out of there, in the middle of winter. And they put me in the bull gang in the north yard. But they defeated themselves by puttin' us on the bull gang. We became an elite crew in the eyes of the other inmates, and they wanted to keep it as punishment.

I was out on the north yard, and, like I've said, I never hesitated to voice my opinions and I don't today. We'd shovel snow, we'd empty railroad cars with hoppers full of coal—frozen coal. It was a tough, miserable, mean job, but the guys were solid guys, and we were close and had become highly respected by the inmate population, and that's where the tough guys were. And in December, a week or two before Christmas, first Christmas away from home, we had a northeast blizzard. Now, for some reason, the overseer or the guard out there wanted us to shovel snow in the middle of the friggin' blizzard. And I said, "You must be out of your fuckin' mind." This fool wanted us to go out there and shovel snow and I said, "No way." I didn't care what anybody else said. I said, "No." And that was it. I wasn't shovelin' snow, absent a good cause. I said, "It's snowin' faster than we can shovel it. It don't make any sense. Why don't we wait until it stops or lets up a little bit?"

He wasn't having any part of reasonin' with us. He said, "You'll shovel or else."

We said, "Well, show us your 'or else.'"

He said, "Well, I'll send for the captain."

I said, "Well, you'll have to send for him, 'cause I ain't shovelin'. That's it."

He said, "Well, what about the rest of them?"

I said, "I don't care about the rest of the guys, I'm not shovelin'."

Then all of us said we weren't goin' to shovel. This was a good lesson for me too, because they were all gonna stick together. And these were the toughest, best guys in the joint, solidest guys, closest friends, involved in the worst punishments that the place felt they could inflict on them and get away with it. They said, "Yeh, we're stickin' together. That's it. We're not shovelin' this crap."

And he sent for the captain, and the man comes out and he says, "All right, you guys get out there and shovel that snow." And he come right up to my face.

I said, "Hey. I'm not gonna get out there and shovel that snow."

He says, "All right. The rest of you feel the same way?"

They started to get mealy-mouthed, some of 'em. "Well, we don't want to shovel if we can't . . ." blah blah.

He said, "Hey. Forget it. That's it." He says, "All of you who don't want to shovel come over here." He formed a line. "Step over the line if you don't want to shovel." And I jumped over it. I was the first one over. Me and five other guys came out from the whole crew.

So that's it. I was locked up for about six weeks. They red-tagged me, disciplinary lockup. This was the first time I met the warden, to talk to him. He called me up on the disciplinary thing. He used to handle that. This was 1970, 1971. The warden at that time was very paternalistic in his operation of the prison. If you went to him with tears in your eyes and said that he was the only one in the world that could help you, you could bet your boots you'd get all the help he could give ya, 'cause he loved that. But that's bootlickin'. I don't think people should have to do that. What about the people that don't know how? He's left out in the shuffle. That's not fair. Anyway, I got called into his office. It just so happened that the guy that would succeed him as warden was there. He had come from Illinois. Well, that was quite a unique experience. They questioned me on it, and I honestly told 'em why I didn't want to shovel snow during a northeast blizzard, and I wasn't tryin' to be smart about it or arrogant or anything else. I just said, "Well, for cryin' out loud. It was a northeast blizzard."

He said, "Well, we'll decide that. We'll decide where you work and when you work."

I said, "Well, you didn't in that case. I decided."

He says, "Well, we gotta get the snow out of there and get the oil trucks in."

I says, "Look, I told the captain when he come out there, if there was an emergency I'd shovel snow around the clock, I'd be the last one to complain or quit if it was necessary. If there was an emergency, I'd go out there and stay until I dropped."

He says, "Well, you seem to do a lot of thinkin' on your own." He says, "I'll have you know that as long as you're here, we'll do your thinkin' for you."

I says, "You think so, huh?" I says, "Well, I'm tellin' you right now that that's where you and I part company. The day you think for me is the day I'll die." I says, "I'll never give in to that. If it's gonna cause us trouble, then so be it. It can start today." I says, "Because you are dead wrong about that. You might be the warden, the keeper of my body, but you got nothin' to do with my mind and my soul. You can't have that."

He says, "Well, you ought to submit a little bit. You'd kinda like to be with your family now. It's comin' Christmas." He started to throw in the low blows.

Then the deputy said somethin' about, "Well, he oughta go in the hole."

I said, "Well, I'd like to see the day you see me inside your hole." I said, "You'll never catch me at anything you'll get me inside your hole for. You can get a bunch of goons and grab me and throw me in there, overpower me and do it. But as far as gettin' me according to your own rules, you'll never do it."

He said, "I bet I will." Then he said, "You can go back to your cell now."

21

The next job they gave me was on the tier. I'd clean the tier and feed the people who were idled in on green tag or red tag for disciplinary reasons. I made sure that the people were fed and the trays were picked up and returned.

One day I felt pretty bad. I had felt bad for a couple of days. I was havin' those migraine headaches again. And, as part of the prescribed treatment for that, I was supposed to go lay down when I felt an attack comin' on. I had a slip from the medical department that I could go lay down.

I told the officer I wanted to go lay down. He said, "Sure." There was no discussion on the thing. I just asked him and he told me okay, and I went and laid down. I didn't go to dinner. I was feelin' too sick.

During the noon hour, when the inmates are locked in their cells, another officer, a young one who hadn't been there very long, come up and changed my tag on my cell door. He put a red tag on it. I looked up and asked him what he was doing. I thought he had made a mistake, got a wrong number or somethin'. He says, "I'm red-tagging you." I said, "What's the story? You got the right cell?"

He says, "Yes. It's you. They told me to come up and put a red tag on ya."

I said, "Who told ya?" He gave me the guy's name. I said, "Did he say what for?"

He said, "No."

I said, "Well I'll be damned." So I laid back down, and I knew this guy would be comin' around on the count after the guys were supposed to go out for the afternoon work. He comes around and checks the cells to find out if anyone is idled in or what, make a count. So he came by, and I says, "Hey, what the hell's the story on the red tag on the door?"

He says, "I red-tagged you."

I said, "Oh. You red-tagged me." And we'd just been over the disciplinary procedure for red-taggin' and everything else with the warden. I was part of a committee that was meetin' with the warden and representatives from the legislature and from the governnor's office to discuss these things, so I was very well aware of what was required in the disciplinary procedures, and one of the requirements was that a person wouldn't be red-tagged unless it was absolutely necessary for the security of the prison or the safety of the man himself or other inmates, and I had done nothing that I could think of.

He says, "I red-tagged you."

I said, "What do you mean, you red-tagged me?" I says, "To begin with, you don't have any authority to put on a red tag." I said, "Do you know the rules? The rules clearly state that if you're gonna lock a guy up, you have to get the officer in charge of custody to affix it. You can't put a red tag on anybody."

And he hemmed and hawed.

I says, "Hey. I know what I'm talkin' about. I'm tellin' you." I says, "You're gonna be in trouble." I said, "I advise you to take it off."

He said, "Well, I'm not going to."

I said, "Well, I'm tellin' you, I think you'd better. You're wrong."

So he went down to get the captain to okay him leavin' the red tag on, so he thought he was safe. Then he come back around. I says, "Hey, look, I don't know what you're up to, goofin' off or playin' a joke or what. I don't understand it. I don't know where you're comin' from. I haven't done a thing to warrant disciplinary action, especially bein' red-tagged." I said, "That's reserved for pretty violent things."

He was used to the old ways where you could get red-tagged for not shovelin' snow in a blizzard or for no reason at all, just if the officer wanted arbitrarily to do it, and he was goin' by the old way. He said, "You refused to work."

I said, "You're crazy. I never refused to work in my life but once, and that was in a northeast blizzard, when I first came here." I said, "No way did I refuse to work." I said, "I asked you to open my door so I could go to my cell and you said sure." He didn't warn me not to, he didn't tell me not to or give me an argument. I said, "Man, this is a real bum deal. You're really tryin' to set me up for some reason. But it's not gonna work. I know how to get to the federal courts and I won't hesitate to have you down there."

They left me in there ten days without bein' found guilty of doin' any wrong, and usually that's the maximum punishment in red-tag. So I got the punishment before I even had a hearin' or anything. Then, about the tenth day, I'd already completed my action for a civil rights case in federal court and I had that all in a manila envelope, and an officer came down to get me to go up to the warden's office for a so-called hearing. And the deputy was in there and the warden—the one who was warden at that time—and the captain.

You see, they weren't used to this kind of stuff. Like he asked me where I was goin' with that green notebook. I said, "I'm takin' that into the hearin'."

He said, "What for?"

I said, "Well, this might develop into a federal case and I want to know who's here and what's said and I want to make notes from it."

He said, "You can't do that."

I said, "Who said I couldn't? There's nothin' in the rules about it."

He said, "Well, I've never seen the likes of this in all the time I've been a guard in the prison." He said, "I don't know what this place is comin' to." He said, "I've never heard of such a thing."

The warden started out the hearin'. I had a lot of experience with the warden from when the Jaycees come in and I was a charter member and on the original board of directors of the prison chapter. He started in an official way. "Well, well, well . . . I got this. . . . I got that."

I says, "Hold it. Before we even get started, I want to tell you somethin'. This whole thing is illegal. It's contrary to the disciplinary rules that we've just straightened out." I says, "This whole thing is wrong. It's based on a lie. Your officer's lyin'. I don't even care to discuss it." I says, "As far as I'm concerned, it's goin' into the courts on a civil rights action."

And right away the warden was visibly disturbed by what I said, not in an angry way but in sort of a fearful way. His immediate remark was, "Well, you're not suing me, are you?" He became defensive. And this kind of surprised me, and it gave me a clue that he had been in trouble before through a civil rights action in a court and he knew that it could get pretty hairy. And I found out later that it was true, he had been in trouble like that before in Illinois, but I didn't know that for sure at the time.

I said, "No, I'm not suin' you. You didn't have nothin' to do with it—yet." I says, "If it's straightened out now, there's no need of it goin' into the courts, even though I've already done ten days' punishment for somethin' I didn't do and without benefit of a hearin' or anythin' else." I said, "I've been punished before I was even heard."

He says, "Well, the officer says you refused to work."

I said, "He's a liar. He's an out-an-out liar." I says, "You can bring him right up here, right now, and I'll tell him to his face he's a liar. I don't know what his motives are and I don't care, but it's a lie." I says, "I only refused to work one time and that's when I first saw you, if you recall when you first come in here, and that was in a northeast blizzard."

He said, "Well, that's not what we're here for today."

I said, "I don't care why I'm here." I said, "You do what you want. I know what I'm goin' to do."

He said, "Well, there must be somethin' we can do." And the deputy wouldn't even look at me, the old deputy that wanted me in the hole, he wouldn't even look at me. And the captain was sittin' there fidgetin' and gettin' nervous.

He asked the deputy if he had anything to say. He says, "No, I ain't got nothin' to say, for him or against him." He wouldn't even look at me, kept lookin' out the window.

They sent me out of the room and called me back about five minutes later. And the warden says, "Well." He says, "Ah, perhaps it would be best for a work change, a change in assignment." He says, "I think what I'll do is . . . You're out of red tag. I'll order the red tag removed. And we'll have you see the work board tomorrow for a change in classification, a reassignment."

I says, "Good. What about the discipline report?"

He says, "Well, there is some question." He says, "It won't be counted against ya. Just forget about it. It's void."

So rather than make a big case out of it and argue about the ten days that I'd been locked up that I couldn't recover, I didn't file a writ for the action in the court. And I went in to the work board, and I had a hell of a time with them. The work board then was a classification board and there was twelve to fourteen people in it—a priest, a guy from voc rehab, a guy from industries, and everything else. And I had been there about three years at the time, and I'd done all my testing with voc rehab—my college entrance exams, my psych tests, a full set of tests—and I'd passed all of 'em with flying colors. And I had obtained my G.E.D. I'd done a lot of things in the time I had been there.

I got up before the work board, and they start runnin' a little game. Like they set me in a chair way away from 'em so I'd feel like I'm on trial and I'm isolated. So they're tryin' to play it like it's a very routine change of classification, like I had put in an application for a job change. And I didn't like what they were doin'. It wasn't based on anything except their own personal and selfish interests.

The guy who was chairin' the thing, the classification officer, asked me where I wanted to go. They expected me to say, "Well, it doesn't really matter." And they were talkin' about all kinds of stuff. And they didn't like me being particular about work assignments. So the classification officer made the mistake of sayin', "Hey, wait a minute." He says, "You're not in here as a result of good behavior or anything. You happen to be here as a result of a disciplinary action." He says, "Let's just put the cards right up on the table."

I says, "Good." I says, "That's just what I want. All the cards right on the table." I says, "I'm glad you said that." And I moved my chair right up to the table and joined them. I says, "It's about time we got the cards on the table. Let's keep 'em there." And I told 'em that this wasn't disciplinary, that the red-taggin' was based on a lie, that it was all straightened out and that I was ready to take the thing to court, I had the thing all prepared, I spent ten days of punishment for somethin' I didn't do. I said, "There's your cards on the table."

The priest told me afterwards, he said his hair rose right on the back of his neck. He says, "Finally, you did impress me."

22

I was in prison in New Hampshire a year without hearing anything from Massachusetts about the charges pending against me there. In fact, I was in technical violation of bail from there, 'cause I was arrested in New Hampshire and couldn't meet my trial date, which I think was May 25. And I didn't like that hanging over me so long. I was worried I'd get another severe sentence. So I filed for disposition of the charges against me, and they had 180 days to come up and get me or forget about it for all time. So they waited almost the 180 days, till it almost expired, and they brought me down to Massachusetts in 1971 to answer the charges. There was something like fourteen warrants, involving six armed robberies and related gun charges and one thing and another.

I was down there about a month in the Lawrence jail before they got all their charges accumulated. I wasn't arraigned on all of 'em, and I had to be arraigned. They were consolidating them for one court, for their benefit, to save money and time. And I was kept in the Lawrence jail all that time.

I had a public defender, Massachusetts public defender, who was appointed to take care of the case for me. And he come and told me that the district attorney was gonna recommend somethin' like fifteen to thirty years if I pleaded guilty. I told him, "He's crazy. No way. That's nothing. That's no deal at all." I says, "I'm not gonna plead guilty if he's gonna be that ridiculous." I says, "I'll just hold out for a trial and a separate trial on each and every charge. They'll have to empanel fourteen juries and they'll have to hold fourteen separate trials. If they want to get stinkin' about it, I'm not gonna cooperate and I'll make it as rough for 'em as I can."

"Well," he says, "it looks like they got ya pretty cold turkey on some of 'em. They can make it rough for you."

I said, "I'm doin' ten to twenty years in New Hampshire. I know what rough is. And I'm not gonna fool around with 'em."

He says, "I'll go back and tell 'em."

So he come back down a few days later, and he says, "Well,

the very least that they'll recommend if you plead guilty to the charges is seven to ten years."

And I says, "Man, they're just tryin' to kill me, you know, bury me."

He says, "That's the very least they'll agree to." He says, "I agree with you that it's rough. We'll do what we can in court. But I recommend that you go in and plead guilty. Let me talk things over with the judge." And he took the information down about the things I accomplished since I'd been in the New Hampshire prison, like being on the original board of directors of the Jaycees, involved in some school work and different things. He felt that might make a difference to the judge and in fact the court might not go along with the district attorney's recommendation. He says, "But you're kind of at their mercy."

Well, when the time came, I went into the courtroom and the judge had the bailiff read the charges against me. It took about twenty minutes to read the charges. I was in chains all this time, you know. And the judge didn't like that too much. They brought me in, in the cattle line, everybody chained together with other people that were there for court business that day. And the judge says, "Take those chains off him." This was a real beautiful judge. He says to me, "Come forward. Come on up to the bench. Approach the bench."

So I went up and stood up on the little paddock beside his bench. They had already read the charges against me, for the benefit of the court and the spectators or for the stenographer or whatever. So he said, "Well, we got a lot of work to do here, don't we?"

I said, "Yeah, I'd say so."

So he says, "On this warrant . . ." And he starts readin' off the number and what the charge was. "How do you plead?"

I pleaded guilty. And we're goin' on down the line. I was pleadin' guilty to all of 'em. I didn't have no choice. They had me. They had me.

It was takin' an awful long time, 'cause he had to read 'em and he had to ask me if I understood the charges and if I knew what I was doin' and all of those type things. And, I don't know, somethin' about it started to strike him funny 'cause there was so much of it. And he come to one warrant where I was charged with assault and battery with a deadly weapon. And I said, "Not guilty." This was my first robbery, at the bar, where they claimed that I pistol-whipped 'em, and I pleaded not guilty.

He says, "What do you mean, not guilty?"

I said, "I'm pleadin' guilty to everything that's sensible, where I actually had anything to do with any of the crimes involved."

He says, "Well, these people said that you hit 'em with a weapon. Two of the people, of the seven involved, said you hit 'em with a weapon."

I said, "Your honor, that's a lie, and I'm not pleadin' guilty to it." I says, "I'm not here to anger the court or the prosecution or anybody else, but can you see me goin' in there and committin' that kind of crime and takin' the time to pistol-whip two of the people when any one of 'em could have shot me in the back if I tried it?" I says, "They cooperated. I got what I was after. They gave me the money and I left." I says, "That's all there is to it and I'm not pleadin' guilty to that charge."

He says, "The court finds you not guilty of that charge."

And he's reading along about some more things. And part of the charges against me were possession of a firearm, usin' a firearm in the commission of a crime, and things like that. And he questioned me, "Did you in fact have a gun in your hand?" I was pleadin' guilty to the whole thing, except that assault thing.

Then he come to that one in Haverhill, that payroll robbery. And he read the charge—robbery, assault and battery with a deadly weapon. I said, "Not guilty." I said, "I didn't assault nobody. In fact, I was assaulted. The assault was on me."

He says, "What do you mean?"

So I told him what happened there, how the woman resisted me, slammed the drawer on my hand and scratched me. I told him I had to get out of there before she jumped on my back and scratched my eyes out.

Well, he started laughin'. He turned his head away, I suppose, to maintain the decorum of the court. He says, "If you so much as touch her, even rest your hand against her arm, during a robbery, that satisfies the legal definition of assault and battery with a deadly weapon. That's the law."

I says, "Look. The way you just described it, I'll have to plead guilty, but I want the record to be very clear that I never did hurt anybody. I never took the initiative and inflicted bodily harm or injury on a single soul." I says, "If I touched that woman, it was to protect myself."

He says, "All right. That may be in the record, and it probably should be." He says, "I just want you to know what the law says on it."

I said, "I can just picture somebody readin' that I pleaded guilty to such a crime years from now and thinkin' that I'm some kind of monster. And I want the record to clearly show that that's not the case. In fact, I was the one who was attacked."

He went on and on. Ultimately we came to the end of it, and he filed all of the gun charges. He found me not guilty on the one assault on the two guys that claimed they were pistol-whipped, 'cause that was in fact a lie. I don't know why they did such a thing, maybe just lookin' for sympathy with the police or tryin' to make themselves spectacular in the news or with their buddies. I don't know why people lie when somethin's already bad enough. He filed the one where she had charged me with assault and battery with a deadly weapon. Everything was filed except the actual six armed robberies. And he started readin' those off. He says, "On this one does the state have anything to say before I pass sentence?"

And they got up and they run a big rap about, "Well these are very serious crimes, your honor. We know the man is incarcerated, serving a lengthy sentence in a sister state, but these are serious crimes and the state does ask for cumulative time of seven to fifteen years."

He asked my attorney if the defense had anything to say. My attorney stood up and he was very, very good. He was eloquent and he had all of the facts. He says, "Well, the defense understands that these are serious charges and there is a number of them." He says, "But I don't think the court can fail to recognize that the man is already serving a very large sentence. He's been incarcerated for approximately a year and a half and he has shown every sign of rehabilitation, responding to treatment and being actively engaged in positive things where he's at." He laid down a pretty good rap for the judge, and it was all true. He also said, "He is contrite. I don't think your honor has missed the fact that he is contrite. If any time has to be imposed at all, three to five years would be more than enough."

The judge says, "So ordered. On the first charge, I find the defendant guilty, three to five years to commence after completion of the term currently served in New Hampshire." And he read off the remaining five charges and they were, each one, three to five years to run concurrent with the first one. So it come out that I had six three-to-five-year sentences runnin' together, to commence after I was free to leave New Hampshire on parole.

23

After that happened in Massachusetts, Donna came up and I could see somethin' was wrong. She couldn't look me in the eye. She cried when she left, and I knew what it was, she'd had a boy friend or somebody. She wrote me a letter and said she knew that I knew and she'd send my folks up to explain. She was gettin' married and she hoped that I didn't hold it against her but she just couldn't go on lonely like she was. This was after two and a half years.

I told her I understood, and I wrote her probably seven letters, and it wasn't beggin' and it wasn't pleadin' and it wasn't threatenin'. It was just askin' her to weigh every situation and the religious aspect of the thing. You see, when Mormons marry, it's not for time only, it's for time and all eternity. And when you have a family, it's for time and all eternity. Death doesn't end the family relationship, and I reminded her of that. I said, "If you got to do somethin', I'd much rather see you go out and take an occasional date somewhere, satisfy your needs and keep it away from the home and not get entangled in a long-term situation that could prove troublesome in the future." What I was doin' was givin' her license to go out. But it's rare and it's hard for a woman to do that, most women and especially that kind of a woman. It's too cheap. She just wasn't brought up that way and she's not that way. To me, I think it speaks well of her, although it would have been better for our relationship if she had just gone out and had an occasional affair once in a while when she felt she had to and not have any emotional attachments to the people. But she's not that kind of person.

She's not happy. I know she's not happy. Our daughter, for instance, is a daddy's girl and she's always visiting me. She'll come down with my parents when she can, and she was always layin' a rap on her mother, talkin' about me, about daddy.

There's no forgiveness needed. If she feels like she needs to be forgiven, then I forgive her. But I understand, and that's more important than forgiving. Forgiving, you might harbor grudges, but when you understand, there's no grudges. And I do understand. I'd've been a lot worse than her if it was her incapacitated in some way, in a hospital or a prison or somethin'. I'd've done as much as she did and more. I'd've done worse things than she did. I'd've probably destroyed the relationship completely so that there'd never be any hope for it, in my man ways of doin' things. But she hasn't done that. She hasn't destroyed it.

Even after she got married she came back, and we had a good relationship for quite a while, maybe a year. We corresponded, and she'd visit when she could. It was really beautiful. She knew then that I had gotten involved in my religion and studying what the priesthood is and what my responsibility is in it. And that really pleased her very much, and she saw a different person in me than what she had ever known before. She was pleased, and she was very much impressed, and she told me so. At the same time she was keepin' up her activities in the Church. I told her, I says, "You know the marriage that you're involved in now is not good for our daughter." I says, "You know it can't go any further than the grave even if you stay together with him all your life, unless he becomes a member of the priesthood and makes himself worthy and you and him can go to the temple."

She says, "I know all that." She says, "When I done that, I was away from the Church. I done it out of spite. I done it for my own convenience." She says, "It was wrong for me to do it." She says, "It's not a lasting relationship. I know that. It's more of a convenience type thing. I had to do somethin'. I couldn't handle it much longer all alone."

I says, "Look. I'm not condemning you. I'm just talkin' to you. With your knowledge of the doctrine, the Gospel doctrine, I'm sure you don't want to be involved in a relationship with a man for time only. I know you think about the family unit more than that."

She said, "Well, I'd rather not get into that right now until you're outa here, and maybe we can make some plans."

And that's pretty much the way it stayed, but then she got to feelin' guilty about seein' me while she was married to him, and she begun to wonder if it wasn't an adulteress type thing, which I disagreed with, 'cause talking doesn't constitute adultery. I said, "It's what's in your mind that might constitute adultery."

She said, "Well, I can't stand bein' there and comin' to see you too. I can't do both." And she says, "If I do break up that situation, what if I get weak again?" She says, "I might become a worse person than I am now."

I saw the wisdom in that. So I agreed to it. And I fully intend to provide for her an opportunity to have a marriage for all time and eternity, if she wants it. I intend to become worthy and, in fact, to be active in my priesthood, and then it'll be up to her to make the decision about what she wants—does she want a life-time situation or somethin' that could go on for all time and eternity?

So she felt guilty, and that guilt forced her to stop comin' to see me. It's been about a year since I've seen her. My sister'll tell her I'm fine and doin' well, and my sister'll come and visit and say she saw her. She still speaks of me. She still thinks of me. She lives in Maine.

24

I've developed a lot in prison. I've had some time to do some thinking about religion and the law and other things. But still I think that prison is a crime. The prisons should be turned into museums so that people can see how people can degrade their fellow human beings. Instead of tryin' to help them and treat them, you make people feel that they're less than human.

I don't think we need any prisons. That's my philosophy. 'Cause if you harm me and if you harm a hundred people, sooner or later you're gonna get yours. We don't need man interferin' in it, with his phony courts and his phony police and his phony prisons, makin' it worse. If you didn't tamper with it, there is such a thing as natural justice. Think back when you was a kid in school and there was the bullies. What ultimately happened to 'em? They didn't do too much damage 'fore they got tuckered down a peg or two. All by itself. I can't hurt nobody without payin' for it. I believe that. And I don't think that I can do good without bein' rewarded for it. I think that is natural, perfect, eternal justice, and that's come to me since I've been here in prison. My eyes have been opened to that. Look at all things on the earth and see if there isn't some kind of natural balance that is far superior to anything man can devise. So society in fact would be doin' itself a great service to tear down its prisons and not interfere so much with natural justice. Some of these people in here in prison are bein' treated far better than they should be, better than they would be if natural justice came down on 'em. You're preventing that, but you're also punishing far greater than you should be, more than is necessary, with this system.

At the point that I went into the prison, it seemed like something very dear, almost like a loved one, had died. Something had died but I never went to its funeral. It's hard to explain. Maybe it's the closeness with the wife, the family, bein' with the kids and, when they are hurt, cuddle them and then treat them, take 'em to bed at night, the visits with the family to the beach. It seemed like all that kind of thing and all the beautiful things died. I can't have a feelin' in me now about them comin' back.

Postscript

Warren Hart was released from prison on parole in February 1977. He has since worked as a pressman for a small printing firm, the manager of a cocktail lounge, the caretaker of an old farm, and manager and performer in a country and western band. He is now training for an executive position in a research and development corporation in New Jersey. While managing the cocktail lounge, he began dating a young woman employed there as bookkeeper. They have since married and recently had a baby girl.

LIBRARY OF CONGRESS CATALOGING IN PUBLICATION DATA

Greenberg, Norman, 1945–
  The man with a steel guitar.

  1. Hart, Warren, 1934– 2. Crime and criminals—
New Hampshire—Biography.   I. Title.
HV6248.H23G73   364.1′552′0924 [B]   79-63084
ISBN 0-87451-175-5

HV6248.H23G73   364.1′552′0924 [B]   79-63084
ISBN 0-87451-175-5